A COZY BOOK OF COFFEES AND COCOAS

RICH AND DELICIOUS RECIPES

Susann Geiskopf-Hadler

D0564816

PRIMA PUBLISHING

PRIMA PUBLISHING and its colophon, which consists of the letter P over PRIMA, are trademarks of Prima Communications, Inc.

Library of Congress Cataloging-in-Publication Data

Geiskopf-Hadler, Susann
   A cozy book of coffees & cocoas : rich and delicious recipes /
Susann Geiskopf-Hadler.
     p. cm.
   Includes index.
   ISBN 0-7615-0121-5
   1. Coffee brewing. 2. Coffee. 3. Cocoa. I. Title.
TX817.C6G45   1995
641.8'77—dc20   95-31381
                                         CIP

96 97 98 AA 10 9 8 7 6 5 4 3 2
Printed in the United States of America

How to Order:

Single copies may be ordered from Prima Publishing, P.O. Box 1260BK, Rocklin, CA 95677; telephone (916) 632-4400. Quantity discounts are also available. On your letterhead, include information concerning the intended use of the books and the number of books you wish to purchase.

Contents

Recipe Listing

Mocha Mint Shake, 81
Iced Cappuccino, 82
Iced Caramel Cappuccino, 82
Iced Raspberry White Choco-
    late Mocha, 83
Iced Caramel Mocha, 84
Vanilla Hazelnut Spritzer, 84

Coffee with Spirits

Coffee with Brandy, 85
Irish Coffee, 86
Kahlua Cream Soda, 86
Homemade Kahlua, 87
Canadian Coffee, 88

Hot Chocolate Drinks

Orange Spice Hot Chocolate, 91
Steamed Hot Chocolate, 92
Mexican Hot Chocolate, 92
Classic Hot Cocoa, 93

Cold Chocolate Drinks

Chocolate Malted Milk, 94
Chocolate Milk with Raspberry
    Syrup, 94

Milk Frothed with Chocolate
    and Mint, 95
Double Chocolate Almond
    Shake, 96
Iced Mexican Chocolate with
    Kahlua, 96

Tasty Treats from the Oven

Blueberry Spice Coffee
    Cake, 102
Blueberry Muffins, 104
Banana Nut Bread, 105
Chocolate Cardamom Bundt
    Cake, 106
Cranberry Scones, 108
George's Cheese Cake, 110
Oatmeal and Chocolate Chip
    Cookies, 112
Espresso Cinnamon
    Brownies, 114
Chocolate Walnut
    Biscotti, 116
Chocolate Espresso
    Cake, 118

Acknowledgments

The writing of this book was sheer indulgence—and what a pleasure it was. Thank you, Jennifer Bayse Sander for conceptualizing the idea; The Dunlavy Studio for producing another great cover; Andi Reese Brady for overseeing the rapid production schedule, and Karen Blanco for her marketing efforts.

David Wagner of Rush Haven in Fair Oaks, California, was an immense help to me. Thank you for so eagerly and willingly sharing your wealth of knowledge. Thank you, Yvonne Shanks, for loaning me your extensive collection of cocoa and chocolate books—they were invaluable.

Guy, my husband, once again created fantastic dinners for me while I was busy working on the manuscript. Thank you for learning to cook. My nieces Lindsey and Natalie eagerly tried all of the cocoa and chocolate drinks—and re-tried them until they were just right. My neighbors the Greenlees and the Speakmans were able and willing taste testers for the coffee and espresso drinks; thank you all. And thank you, Bunnie Day, for all of your encouragement and thoughtful comments.

INTRODUCTION

People are very passionate about both coffee and cocoa. Perhaps the unique legendary history surrounding each owes to our ardor. Popular legend has it that ingesting coffee was first discovered by Kaldi, an Ethiopian goat herder, who found his flock frolicking one day among green shrubs bearing red cherries. Struck by their level of activity, Kaldi collected some of the cherries and took them to a nearby monastery. The monks took great interest and prepared a beverage by boiling the berries.

Coffee beans found their way to Arabia and, by the thirteenth century, the Arabs were roasting and grinding the precious bean and then boiling it with water to produce a beverage. Treasuring their find, the Arabs forbade the raw beans to be taken from the country. Their efforts were in vain—by the 1500s raw coffee beans had been smuggled into Turkey, Egypt, and Syria. European traders were introduced to this new stimulating beverage in local coffeehouses. They soon carried coffee beans to the new colonies throughout the world where it thrives to this day.

The legend of cocoa really begins with the Aztec Emperor Montezuma, although earlier in history it was a part of Mayan and Aztec mystical and religious rituals. History documents that Montezuma drank a chocolate elixir—mixed with herbs and pepper—from golden goblets before retiring to his harem.

Perhaps this is how chocolate first gained its reputation as an aphrodisiac.

In 1519 Hernando Cortez, the explorer from Spain, was treated by Montezuma to lavish banquets. He took great interest in this mysterious beverage, as well as in the golden, jeweled goblets in which it was served. When he returned to Spain in 1528, Cortez took both with him. He served the royal court a sugar-sweetened cocoa beverage that the aristocracy embraced with a passion. In the span of one hundred years, cocoa made its way across Europe, and the cocoa plants to plantations throughout the new colonies.

Today we can enjoy the pleasures of coffee and cocoa cuisine, prepared in the comfort of our own cozy kitchens. This book presents useful information and creative recipes geared to expand your enjoyment of these ever-popular ingredients.

Chocolate has been widely associated with notable historic figures. Both Casanova and Madame DuBarry believed that chocolate was conducive to romance, which fueled chocolate's popularity in Europe to new heights.

3

Exotic Pleasures

Reading a mystery written

by a friend

while at my elbow

a cup of rich black hot

coffee

embraces the senses

steaming the window

as outside spring rains

caress swollen buds

encouraging them

to fulfill

the promise of

the dark rare liquid.

—Patricia E. Canterbury

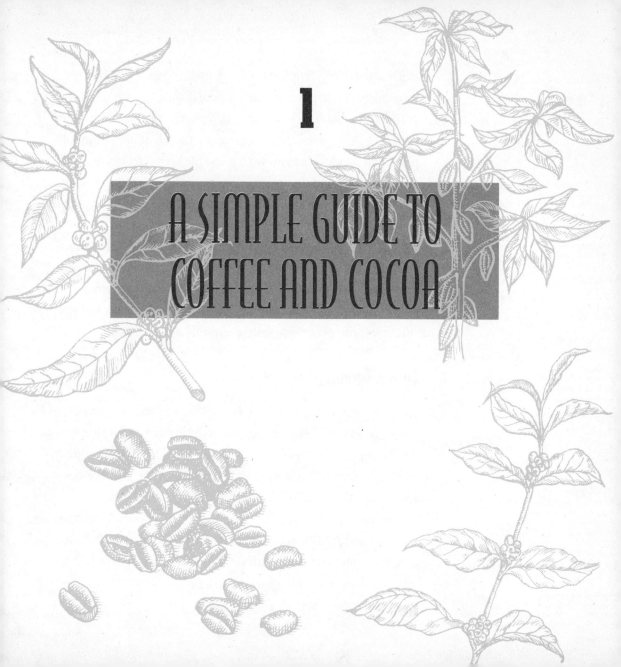

1

A SIMPLE GUIDE TO COFFEE AND COCOA

Within any given tropical coffee-growing region, unique microclimates contribute to the particular qualities found in the coffee bean. Two varieties of coffee plants exist, but from farm to farm, even within the same region, the identical variety of plant will produce a bean with a unique character—much like a vineyard will yield its signature grapes. The roastmaster, like the winemaker, uses his alchemy to produce a distinct finished product.

The cocoa belt also encompasses specific tropical regions. And, like coffee, two distinct varieties of plants exist. Cocoa seeds and coffee beans are both dried before they are roasted. The chocolatier is the counterpart to the roastmaster and presides over the process to create a notable chocolate.

Coffee-Growing Regions

Ethiopia is thought to be the birthplace of coffee, but today coffee trees grow throughout the world in countries that lie within the tropical and subtropical zones. These regions are located roughly 100 miles north and south of the equator between the Tropic of Cancer and the Tropic of Capricorn. Depending on the variety, coffee plantations flourish between sea level and 6,000 feet. Coffee trees require the specific conditions found in these locations. They need a constant temperature range of between 68 and 75 degrees F, rich, well-drained soil, shade, and 60 to 80 inches of rainfall annually. Frequently coffee plantation owners plant banana or coconut trees between the rows of coffee trees to provide shade and mulch, as well as additional income.

The coffee plant, although botanically an evergreen shrub, is usually referred to as a tree. These trees begin to produce 3 to 5 years after they are planted, and continue to produce for about 25 years. The beautiful jasmine-scented white blossom turns into a cherry that ripens from green to yellow to red. The coffee bean is the seed of the ripe fruit, encased by the layers that make up the cherry. The annual yield of each tree is only 1 to 1 1/2 pounds of roasted coffee.

Most coffee cherries host two coffee beans; but occasionally only one bean forms, and that bean is called a *peaberry*. Coffee from peaberries tends to be lighter in body and flavor than coffee from the high-grade normal beans from the same tree. Usually the peaberry coffee is sold by the name of the country in which it originates, such as Tanzanian Peaberry.

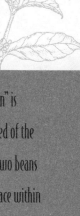

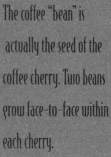

The coffee "bean" is actually the seed of the coffee cherry. Two beans grow face-to-face within each cherry.

Types of Coffee Plants

Arabica and robusta are the two species of coffee plants that grow throughout the world, giving us a myriad of unique coffees.

Coffee Arabica

Arabica beans derive their name from Arabia—the ancient name for Yemen—where they are believed to have originated. These mountain-grown beans thrive in altitudes between about 2,000 and 6,000 feet and produce about 75 percent of the world's coffee. This species is grown predominately in Central America, South America, eastern Africa, and Indonesia. All specialty coffees come from the arabica beans.

The cherries of the arabica variety usually do not ripen at the same time, requiring the pickers to selectively pick and to make repeat trips to the same trees. Once picked, the cherries are generally processed by a wet-wash method. A machine breaks away the cherries' outside skin and pulp, exposing a sticky coating called *mucilage* that encases the parchment-covered beans. The beans are placed in large tanks of water for about 24 hours to ferment, then removed and thoroughly washed. They are dried in the sun for two to three days, then placed in a milling machine that removes most of the parchment to expose the green beans.

The wet-processed arabica beans tend to have a bright, clean, clear flavor. Once roasted, the unique characteristics develop. Delicate and flavorful, with a balanced aroma and sweet yet acidic taste are some of the characteristics used to describe

About four thousand hand-picked beans comprise a single pound of specialty coffee.

this bean. Each growing region has its own unique qualities that come through in the roasted bean.

Coffee Robusta

Robusta bean varieties grow at elevations between sea level and 2,000 feet and flourish in the wet valley lands and humid tropical forests. Most of the plantations are located in West Africa and Indonesia. These plants tend to be more disease-resistant than the arabica species.

The cherries from the robusta trees ripen all at once, allowing them to be dry-processed. They are left on the trees to partially dry, then harvested and spread out in the sun. The cherries are raked several times a day for two to three weeks until completely dry. They are then put through a hulling machine to remove the dried pulp, parchment, and silver skin. The resulting beans are greenish to brownish in color.

Robusta beans have about twice the caffeine content of arabicas. Most robusta beans are used to produce instant coffee or commercial blends.

Types of Coffee Roast

Coffee beans, when green, have little flavor and are almost as hard as rocks. Roasting brings out their sugars, oils, proteins, and minerals. The country of origin, the environmental conditions during growing and harvesting, and the method of processing used all contribute to the resulting flavor.

Excellent flavors also depend on the skills of an experienced roastmaster. The intense heat produced by the roasting equipment—usually between 435 to 485 degrees F—triggers a complex chemical reaction within the green beans, causing them to pop and nearly double in size. As they lose their moisture, the sugars and starches are transformed into the volatile oils that are responsible for most of the flavor and aroma. Decisions about how quickly and how darkly to roast are in the hands of the roastmaster. Roasting time ranges from 12 to 15 minutes.

The degrees of roast can be broken down into basic categories. Although there is no standard terminology used throughout the industry, these categories will help you understand the flavor differences.

Light Roast Lightly roasted coffees are cinnamon in color and characteristically have intense aromas, with crisp acidity and sourness as the dominate flavor note. They tend to have a light, undeveloped body. Most commercially canned coffee is lightly roasted.

> I like my coffee black as the devil, hot as hell, pure as an angel, and sweet as love.
>
> —Talleyrand

Medium Roast   Medium roast beans—also known as "city" or "full city"—are chestnut in color with a perfect balance of body and acidity. The beans' distinguishing characteristics are prevalent. This roast brings out the full range of flavors and is used by most specialty roastmasters.

Dark Roast   In this roast the beans, as the name implies, are a dark bittersweet chocolate brown in color and have a subtle trace of oil on the surface. The acidity is replaced with a slightly roasty bitterness and pungent flavor. The varietal characteristics are masked, emphasizing this bolder, smoky taste. Espresso and Italian roast fall into this category.

Very Dark Roast   The color of very dark roasted beans is dark brown to black, and the surface of the bean is oily. The primary flavor is that of carbony bitterness, without much body. This roast flavor is the most dominate quality of French roast coffee.

Interestingly enough, darker roast coffees have slightly less caffeine than the lighter roasts because the longer the beans are roasted, the more moisture is removed. Caffeine is part of that moisture and accounts for the oily surface of the beans. An espresso does not contain more caffeine than a cup of commercially roasted coffee, but it does have a stronger, more intense flavor.

Cocoa-Growing Regions

It is believed that the jungles of the Amazon produced the first cocoa trees. Centuries ago, the trees were transported from there to the Yucatan peninsula by the Mayans who cultivated cocoa as a crop. The trees flourish in tropical areas—the cocoa belt—that lie 20 degrees north and south of the equator. Most plantations are located in Africa, South and Central America, and parts of Asia. Cocoa trees require intense heat and moisture. The plants must also be sheltered from the wind and from direct sunlight, so other trees such as banana and rubber are frequently planted to protect them.

The botanical name for the cocoa tree is *Theobroma cocoa*—food of the Gods. This wide-branching tropical evergreen tree will grow as tall as 60 feet in its natural setting; however, on plantations it is usually pruned to about 20 feet. The trees begin to bear fruit when they are 3 to 5 years old and continue to produce for 30 to 40 years.

Cocoa trees produce a cluster of waxy white blossoms that have a slightly pink blush. The blossoms hang on short stalks off the main trunk or on heavy branches that are near the trunk. They turn into green or maroon pods measuring 6 to 14 inches long and two to five inches wide. When ripe, these pods range from golden to earthy red in color. Flowers and pods are produced simultaneously throughout the year; when the pods are harvested, special care must be taken so the flowers are not damaged. This delicate harvest takes place twice a year on commercial plantations. It takes 400 dried seeds—the beans within the pods—to yield a pound. The average tree produces one to two pounds of cured seeds (beans) annually.

A cocoa tree sprouts thousands of tiny waxy pink or white blossoms, but only 3 to 10 percent mature into full fruit.

Types of Cocoa Plants

Forasteros and Criollos are the two basic species of cocoa plants, although many hybrids have been developed.

Forasteros

This species grows primarily in West Africa and Brazil. They are hearty plants and are characterized by their thick-walled pods. The cured seeds of this variety are often used by chocolatiers as the base bean and blended with other more flavorful varieties.

Criollos

Criollos produce a thin-skinned pod that hosts a seed noted for its concentrated flavor. A more delicate plant, Criollos thrive in Java, Samoa, Venezuela, Sri Lanka, and Madagascar. These beans produce the finest quality products and are noted for their aromatic quality.

Once harvested, both varieties are processed the same way. The large pods are cracked open to expose from 20 to 50 white, cream, or lavender-colored seeds that are embedded in a white or pink pulp. The seeds and pulp are scooped out of the pods and placed in the sun. The pulp ferments away in two to three days, leaving seeds that are then put into baskets or boxes to ferment for an additional three to nine days. This fermentation process removes the bitter acid and develops the essential oils, turning the seeds into a dark brown bean.

The beans are then dried before they are packaged for shipping. Most often they are spread on trays or bamboo matting and dried in the sun. In more moist climates, the beans are dried indoors by hot-air pipes. Either method takes several days, during which time the beans are turned frequently.

Roasting Cocoa

Dried cocoa beans are stored in warehouses, filling them with a poignant, exotic aroma. The beans are cleaned and sorted for size, then various types of beans are secretly blended to create each manufacturer's unique concoction.

Trinitario is believed to be a natural cross strain of the criollo and forastero species of cocoa plants. These trees are particularly suitable for cultivation.

Next the beans are roasted in large rotary cylinders for 30 minutes to two hours at temperatures ranging between 250 and 350 degrees F. The chocolatier presides over the roasting, determining the temperature and degree of roast. This stage of the process is much like that performed by the coffee roast-master. As with coffee beans, the cocoa beans develop their characteristic aroma, flavor, and color when roasted.

After roasting, the warm beans are placed in a machine that breaks off the outer shells revealing the *nib*—small pieces of the bean. These nibs contain 50 to 54 percent cocoa butter. The nibs are then crushed between steel or stone disks. This process, known as conching, generates heat that liquefies the cocoa butter—most of which is removed—yielding the chocolate liquor, a thick dark cocoa paste. This chocolate liquor is the base ingredient from which all other forms of chocolate are made.

Cocoa manufacturers carefully guard the three critical factors in chocolate making: proportions of ingredients, temperatures, and time intervals.

Give me the luxuries of life and I will
willingly do without the necessities.
—Frank Lloyd Wright

2

CHOOSING AND STORING COFFEE AND COCOA

Fresh, premium-quality beans are essential to brewing an excellent cup of coffee or espresso. Try to purchase your beans directly from a roaster or high-traffic coffee retailer to ensure optimum freshness.

In today's marketplace, many different coffees are available. There are varietal or straight coffees that are named after the country of their origin, special blends of coffee, and even flavored coffees. Many are also available in a decaffeinated form. Armed with some knowledge, it is easy to choose specialty beans and enjoy the subtle differences each one offers.

Cocoa and chocolate products are more closely distinguished by their manufacturer's specific formula. To achieve delicious results at home, it is essential to choose the right cocoa or chocolate for the right purpose. The specific types—bittersweet, milk chocolate, or cocoa—all have their places in chocolate cuisine. Unlike roasted coffee, chocolate products have a relatively long shelf life, and though the appearance may be affected by hot and cold temperatures, chocolate does not loose its aroma or flavor.

Selecting Coffee Beans

Flavor Terminology

The terms used to describe coffee's particular characteristics are similar to those associated with fine wines and are almost endless. The four most important—in addition to the types of roast discussed in chapter 1—are aroma, body, acidity, and flavor.

- ❖ AROMA. This is the fragrance that our senses first detect when presented with freshly brewed coffee. It is distinctive and often complex. The brew may be described as carmelly or carbony; fruity or floral; or perhaps herby or spicy.
- ❖ BODY. The body describes how coffee feels on the tongue. It can range from thin and watery, to oily or thick, to buttery or syrupy. This varies depending on the type of bean and the brewing method used.
- ❖ ACIDITY. The acidity in coffee is not synonymous with bitter or sour and does not refer to its actual acid level—on the pH scale, coffee is relatively low. Rather, it notes the refreshing, brisk, lively qualities that make coffee a palate-cleansing beverage.
- ❖ FLAVOR. The term flavor is the overall impression and includes the aroma, body, and acidity of the coffee. A particular coffee may be described as having a nut-like aroma, chocolate-like taste, and a smooth refreshing finish.

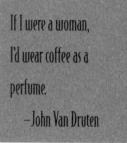

If I were a woman,
I'd wear coffee as a
perfume.
    –John Van Druten

Specific Regional Characteristics

There are many coffee beans available from specialty coffee retailers. Coffee beans—like wine grapes—develop certain

characteristics specific to the region in which they grow. The soil, sun, and rain all interplay to affect the flavors and body of the bean. Some specific guidelines will help you select coffees to brew at home.

The Americas

Beans from the Americas tend to be light- to medium-bodied, with clean lively flavors. Some of the more popular include Brazil Santos, Colombia Supremo, Guatemala Antigua, Costa Rica Tarazu, Mexico Altura, and Kona.

Brazil Santos   Brazil is the world's largest coffee producer; the industry began there in the early 1720s. The beans are generally processed by the dry method. The resulting light-bodied coffee is dry and mildly acidic with a sweet tasting finish.

Colombia Supremo   Jesuit missionaries first brought coffee to Colombia in 1808, and legend has it that Father Romero encouraged his flock to plant the trees as a form of penance. Today, Colombia is the world's second largest coffee producer. Columbian beans brew a mildly aromatic coffee that has a smooth caramel taste. Medium-bodied and nicely balanced, it is also used in many coffee blends.

Coffee is big business; it is second only to oil as a commodity on world markets.

Costa Rica Tarazu   Introduced from Cuba in 1779, Costa Rican coffees are a popular choice among serious coffee drinkers. The tangy aroma, complex, slightly fruity taste and medium body earn this coffee a well-rounded reputation.

Guatemala Antigua   Grown in the high elevations of the Antigua region, this coffee is very aromatic with a dry, nutty flavor and mild texture. It is considered by many to be the best of the Central American varieties.

Mexico Altura   This coffee is grown in southern Mexico on the high slopes of the Sierras. The fragrant aroma, hazelnut flavor, and light body make this well-balanced coffee delicious for breakfast with cream and sugar.

Kona   King Kamehameha II brought the first coffee plant to the islands in 1827 after a visit to England. Intended to be ornamental, the plant thrived in the volcanic soil, giving rise to the industry. The Kona coast of the big island of Hawaii—and more recently parts of Kauai—are the only places in the United States that commercially produce coffee. Grown on the slopes of the Mona Loa and Hualalai volcanoes, Kona coffee is delicately aromatic, mild in flavor, and well balanced.

The plantation that I visited in Kona was on the slopes of Mona Loa. Mango trees were neatly planted in rows to provide the necessary shade for the coffee trees. A cup of Kona always takes me back to the islands.

–the author

21

East Africa and Yemen

East Africa and Yemen produce beans that have a sparkling acidity with floral, fruity, or winy flavor notes and a medium- to full-body. Ethiopia Sidamo, Kenya AA, Mocha, and Zimbabwe are my favorite coffees from this region.

Ethiopia Sidamo   Arabica coffee is native to Ethiopia, believed to be the birthplace of coffee. Sidamo is the high-plateau growing district in south-central Ethiopia. The beans are blue-green in color before roasting, yielding a coffee that is low acid, full bodied, with a floral aroma and sumptuous aftertaste. This is my favorite everyday coffee.

Kenya AA   Many of the beans grown in Africa are the low-elevation robusta variety, but this arabica coffee is grown high on the slopes of Mt. Kenya. The AA designation refers to the size of the bean—AA is the largest, followed by an A and B grade. Kenya coffee has a ripe blackberry aroma, with a dry winy taste, crisp acidity, and medium-bodied richness.

Mocha   This coffee is organically grown in the mountains of Yemen, much as it was over a thousand years ago. It gained its name from the ancient port of Mocha through which it was originally shipped. Mocha is a distinctive coffee with a light winy acidity and a rich chocolaty aftertaste. This balanced coffee is frequently blended with Java, a bean from Indonesia.

Zimbabwe　Formerly Rhodesia, this country produces a coffee known for its fruity, well-balanced flavor and delightful spicy aftertaste. It is not as easy to find as some of the other African coffees, but it is worth the search.

Indonesia

Coffees grown in Indonesia are usually full-bodied but smooth, and low in acidity. Their flavor is described as earthy and exotic. These coffees are delicious with milk or cream. Look for Celebes, Java, New Guinea, and Sumatra Mandheling.

Where coffee is served there is grace and splendor.

—anonymous

Celebes　This low acid, highly aromatic coffee is named for the former Dutch colony that was located on the small island of Sulawesi, where it is grown. The bean is in short supply—considered one of the world's finest coffees, it commands a high price. The coffee is characterized by its smooth, rich, slightly smoky taste with full body and sweet finish.

Java　The Dutch first planted coffee trees on the island of Java in 1696, and to this day the term Java is synonymous with coffee. This full, rich-bodied coffee with nicely balanced acid and a complex spicy aroma is delicious on its own, but you will frequently find it blended with the African Mocha bean.

New Guinea   Coffee plants were introduced to New Guinea from Jamaica in the 1930s. They grow in the tropical rugged mountain highlands of Papua on the eastern half of the island. The coffee has a rich pungent and tangy quality with a medium body.

Sumatra Mandheling   This coffee is grown high in the mountains of west-central Sumatra, near the port of Padang. It is characterized by its herbal aroma, extremely full body, heavy rich smooth flavor, and gentle acidity.

Blends and Flavored Coffees

Many specialty coffee retailers offer their own blends. Blends of similar types of coffee allows the roastmaster to blend the green beans before roasting. Different types of coffees must be blended after roasting so that each individual type of bean can be custom-roasted to achieve its optimum flavor. Blending beans creates greater complexity and distinctive customized flavors. Try different ones to see what you like.

Arabica beans that are low acid and not bitter are usually selected for flavored coffees. Spices are often added to freshly roasted beans. The roastmasters may also apply flavoring oils or powders to freshly roasted beans while they are still hot and absorbent.

When grinding flavored beans at home, be sure to thoroughly clean your grinder after each use so any residue of flavor is not transferred to the next batch of beans you grind. Use a stiff brush to brush away all the grounds. Alternately, grind through a small batch of unflavored stale beans, then discard them. They will absorb any residual flavoring.

If you want to improve your understanding, drink coffee.

—Sydney Smith

Decaffeinated Coffee

There is much information, and misunderstanding, surrounding caffeine. Basically, caffeine is a mild stimulant that is found occurring naturally as a compound in over 60 species of plants and trees. We most commonly ingest it when consuming coffee, tea, chocolate, and cola drinks, as well as in prescription drugs and headache pills.

Individual tolerance to caffeine varies widely, but for most individuals moderate daily consumption poses no problems. Caffeine works as a gentle assistant to thought, productivity, and conversation.

Decaffeinated coffee has had 97 percent of the caffeine removed, leaving most of the flavors intact. Different methods are employed in this process—primarily of European origin—but all begin with green beans. The most common technique immerses the beans in warm-to-hot water. The beans swell in size opening up the cellular structure, which brings the caffeine to the surface where it mixes with the water. The beans are drained and the water is treated with a solvent—the safest and most common is methylene chloride—that extracts the caffeine but leaves most of the beans' flavorful oils intact. The water is returned to the beans for re-absorption of the oils. The beans are then rinsed and dried. The extracted caffeine is not disposed of, but rather sold to beverage and pharmaceutical companies. Any trace of the solvent that might possibly remain in the green beans is highly volatile, vaporizing at 104 degrees F. Since the green beans are then roasted at a minimum of at least 400 degrees F for about 15 minutes, it is highly unlikely that any trace of the solvent would remain.

Swiss Water Process is another commonly used technique. The green beans are submersed in extremely hot water, then the water is percolated through activated charcoal. The beans are then returned to the water where they reabsorb the flavorful oils. This process yields a slightly more expensive bean since the extracted caffeine cannot be removed from the charcoal and sold as a by-product for use in colas or pharmaceutical products.

Storing Coffee Beans

Fresh premium-quality beans are essential to a great cup of coffee, no matter how you brew it. Unfortunately, roasted coffee beans—whole or ground—have a short shelf life. Moisture, heat, and air cause the flavorful oils and fats in the beans to oxidize after roasting.

Whole beans retain their freshness longer than ground because not as much surface area is exposed. Ground coffee begins to deteriorate within a few hours but remains mostly unaffected for about a week. The aroma is the first thing that disappears, followed by some of the flavor. Although drinkable, the coffee will lack its unique characteristics. Experts recommend purchasing whole beans in small quantities and using them within two to three weeks. Store whole beans—or, if you must, ground coffee—in an airtight container in a cool, dark place. Coffee may be stored in the freezer for longer periods; however, do not take coffee in and out of the freezer. This causes condensation to build up on the beans, which destroys the flavor of the coffee.

For the ultimate cup, seek out a coffee retailer that also roasts their own beans and make a point of visiting them weekly for your coffee purchases. Grind your coffee at home immediately before brewing it.

Selecting and Storing Cocoa and Chocolate

Chocolate liquor is the base ingredient in all forms of chocolate. The amount of cocoa butter in the finished product distinguishes the different types of chocolate. Powdered cocoa and solid-bar chocolate both have distinctive characteristics and specific uses.

Unlike coffee, each type of chocolate has slightly different storage requirements. In general, however, chocolate should be stored in a cool, dry place—68 to 78 degrees F is ideal. When stored at cold temperatures, such as in the refrigerator or freezer, chocolate will sweat when brought to room temperature. In too warm a temperature, the chocolate will develop a pale color on its exterior—a bloom. This happens when a slight amount of the cocoa butter separates and rises to the surface. The chocolate itself is not spoiled, just its appearance.

Cocoa butter is the fat that occurs naturally in cocoa beans. It gives chocolate its particular smoothness and melt-in-the-mouth texture.

Types of Cocoa and Chocolate

Cocoa powder   This is pulverized chocolate liquor. Most of the cocoa butter has been pressed out during processing, yielding a product containing only 10 to 24 percent cocoa butter. It is convenient to use in baking or beverages since it does not have to be melted. There are two types of cocoa powder, natural and Dutch process. The natural cocoa powder—meaning nonalkalized—has a strong chocolate flavor and medium-brown color. Coenraad van Houten, a Dutchman, invented the Dutching machine that treats the cocoa with an alkali to neutralize the natural acidity. Most European cocoas are Dutch process. They have a slightly milder flavor and darker chocolate color. Stored in a tin away from moisture, cocoa powder will last for years.

Unsweetened chocolate   Sometimes called baking chocolate, unsweetened chocolate is chocolate liquor that has been molded into blocks and hardened. It contains no sugar and thus has a bitter taste. The content of cocoa butter in this form of chocolate ranges between 50 and 58 percent, depending on the blend of cocoa beans used. Unsweetened chocolate is frequently used for making brownies, fudges, and frostings. Look for it in packages of eight individually wrapped one-ounce

The creator of milk chocolate was a chemist named Henri Nestle. In researching milk products for babies allergic to mother's milk, he discovered sweet condensed milk, which was a byproduct of an experiment. This attracted the attention of Swiss chocolatier Daniel Peter, who in 1876, employed Nestle to make the first milk chocolate.

portions. This chocolate will keep indefinitely if stored well wrapped in a cool, dry place.

Semisweet and bittersweet chocolate   Both of these contain chocolate liquor, additional cocoa butter, sugar, vanilla or vanillin, and lecithin. These chocolates are delicious to eat and may be used interchangeably in recipes, although bittersweet is generally slightly stronger in chocolate flavor and slightly less sweet than semisweet. Store bittersweet and semisweet chocolate well wrapped in a cool, dry place for up to 12 months.

Chocolate chips   These yummy morsels are usually made from semisweet chocolate but are also available in milk chocolate and white chocolate forms. The chocolate is specially formulated to be used in chocolate chip cookies and other recipes where it is important for the chocolate to remain in chip form rather than to melt completely. Do not substitute chocolate chips in recipes calling for its solid counterpart.

Milk chocolate   This chocolate, as any child will tell you, is best for eating. It has a mild flavor and soft texture due to its milk solids and low chocolate liquor content. Milk chocolate is not good for baking, as it cannot tolerate even moderate heat without burning. Milk chocolate does not store well, so enjoy it shortly after you purchase it.

Chocolate syrup   Chocolate syrup is cocoa powder, water, granulated sugar, salt, and vanilla. Hershey makes a great one and, refrigerated, it will keep indefinitely.

White chocolate   Technically not chocolate at all—it contains no chocolate liquor—authentic white chocolate is ivory in color and made from cocoa butter, sugar, milk solids, lecithin, and vanilla or vanillin. In solid form, it has a creamy texture with a faint chocolate aroma and smooth taste. It does not tolerate high heat, so is usually not used for cooking or baking. Powdered white chocolate is also available and is a pleasant addition to coffee beverages. White chocolate has a very short shelf life, so make sure that it is fresh when you purchase it and use it immediately.

Choosing Quality Cocoa and Chocolate
Some chocolate houses and candy shops will allow you to sample chocolate before you purchase it. This is an especially enjoyable task, but there are some things that you should be looking for.

My figure is the result of a lifetime of chocolate eating.
    – Katherine Hepburn

- ❖ SIGHT. Sight is the first thing to observe. Fresh chocolate should have a glossy shine. A whitish powdery bloom on the surface indicates that the chocolate has been stored at too high of a temperature.

- ❖ SMELL. The smell is next; it should be fresh and moist. The chocolaty aroma will be sweet or bitter depending on the type of chocolate.

- ❖ TOUCH. When touched, the surface of the chocolate should be cool and moist. After a few minutes in the hand, it should begin to melt. White chocolate or milk chocolate will melt the fastest.

- ❖ SOUND. When a bar of chocolate is broken you should hear a crisp snap and the break should be clean, not crumbly.

- ❖ TASTE. When placed in the mouth, the chocolate should melt evenly on the tongue and excite the taste buds.

- ❖ TEXTURE. Powdered cocoa should have a consistent, powdery appearance and a rich chocolaty aroma.

National Characteristics of Cocoa and Chocolate

Tastes in cocoa and chocolate seem to be a national thing—over the centuries each country that produces chocolate has developed its signature flavor. The chocolatiers guard their formulas carefully, but—luckily for us—they do export their finished products to the United States.

Belgium Belgium is world-renowned for its outstanding chocolate. Specialty chocolate houses are found on every town square, the fragrance wafting out the door. Their chocolate tends to be rich and full-flavored. Handmade, filled chocolates are a specialty. Look for Beuhaus, Cote d'or, and Godiva.

France Most French chocolate is made from cocoa beans grown in the former French West African colonies. As is the French way, special attention is given to chic packaging that, once opened, reveals dark, aromatic chocolate. Fouquet, Pierre, and Koenig are beautifully presented and the most widely available.

Germany German chocolate—not to be confused with the brand name commonly used in baking—is renowned for being rich, oily, and sweet. Mondose and Ruber are notable.

Italy The Italians like things to be attractively presented, and this fact has not been overlooked when it comes to their chocolates. Their offerings are frequently studded with nuts that are grown in northern Italy. Seek out Pernigotti, Perugina, or Rondo.

I well remember my indulgence that cold April morning, on the ancient town square of Brussels.
—the author

Mexico   Mexican chocolate is ground with cinnamon—and sometimes almonds—producing a unique, aromatic cocoa. Small hexagon-shaped cakes are also made, with sugar added. Look for Ibarra, Presidencial, or Morelia.

Netherlands   Most of their cocoa beans come from the former Dutch colonies of Indonesia. The resulting chocolate is noted for being rich and hearty. Holland is particularly recognized for its cocoa powder, Droste and Van Houten being most available.

Switzerland   Swiss chocolates are usually associated with creamy, smooth milk chocolate bars, although beautifully wrapped bittersweet chocolate bars—flat and triangular in shape—are also produced. Seek out Lindt and Tobler.

United Kingdom   British chocolatiers are most noted for their mint chocolates. The Brits also like sweet dark chocolate and rich milk chocolate. Cadbury and Joseph Terry are delicious.

United States   Americans have many different tastes in chocolate, brought by the many immigrants who inhabit this country. The Hershey Chocolate Company of Pennsylvania

As a child living in England, I especially enjoyed Smarties—pastel-colored M&M-like candy sold in a tube.

—the author

began producing chocolate products in the late nineteenth century. The slightly gritty but flavorful chocolate they produced dominated the market for years. Today look for Baker, Ghirardelli, Nestle, and Hershey.

Forrest Mars, son of Frank Mars of Mars, Inc., started his own chocolate company in 1940 with Bruce Murrie. They combined their initials to create M&Ms, a chocolate candy that could be carried without melting. M&Ms became a popular K-ration during World War II.

The London coffeehouse that Edward Lloyd opened in 1688 became the center of maritime intelligence and insurance—and evolved into the well-known Lloyds of London.

3

TOOLS OF THE TRADE

Essential Tools for Making Coffees

There are many gadgets available in specialty stores designed to produce the perfect cup of coffee. Armed with some knowledge, you can purchase appliances that will meet your needs and satisfy your sense of aesthetics. Then you can sit back and enjoy a delicious cup of coffee.

Cocoa and chocolate drinks do not require specific equipment for their preparation beyond a saucepan, whisk, and blender. There are, however, some techniques to master.

Coffee Grinders

The grinding process has evolved throughout the centuries. Early on, the roasted beans were pounded with a mortar and pestle to unlock the flavor within. With the advent of the millstone, the same type of two large wheels used to grind wheat berries were employed to grind coffee. Today, choose from Turkish-style, hand crank, electric blade, or burr grinders.

Turkish-style grinders   These are necessary for brewing Middle Eastern coffee. The grinder resembles a pepper grinder, milling the coffee beans into a fine powdery consistency.

Hand crank grinders   This millstone-type of grinder does not require electricity and can be set for a specific grind, thus producing a consistently ground coffee. Set properly to a fine grind, you can even grind beans to espresso specifications.

Electric blade grinders   These are inexpensive grinders and used in most homes. They whirl two blades at a high speed, chopping the beans into irregular pieces. You determine the type of grind by the length of time you whirl the beans around, not by a predetermined setting. Each machine differs, but the following guidelines may be applied.

French press plunger pots: Coarse grind, about 6 seconds
Flat bottom drip filters: Medium grind, about 10 seconds
Cone shaped drip filters: Fine grind, about 25 seconds
Espresso: Extra fine powderlike grind,
                                           30-plus seconds

It is difficult to produce a grind that is fine enough for espresso with an electric blade grinder. Another drawback to this type of grinder is that the blades can generate a heat that will adversely effect the volatile oils in the beans. To avoid this, grind your beans in spurts, a few seconds at a time.

Coffee is the common man's gold, and like gold, it brings to every man the feeling of luxury and nobility.
     –Abd-al-Kadir, 1587

Burr grinders Although expensive, these grinders produce a uniform grind ranging from coarse to extra fine. The machine is set to a calibrated grade, individually crushing the whole beans. Heat is minimized in the grinding process, leaving the volatile oils undisturbed.

With any type of grinder, it is important to keep it clean. Coffee beans contain oil that does leave a residue. This residue can cause the next batch of beans that you grind to be bitter and can even clog the machine. Use a stiff brush to remove any coffee from the blades or burrs, then take a soft cloth to wipe the bean container and lid clean.

Coffee Brewing Equipment

All brewing equipment has one thing in common—coffee beans come in contact with water to yield a unique beverage. Given the correct water temperature and type and grind of coffee, you will produce a perfect cup. Drip, French press, and espresso are the most popular methods, each calling specific equipment into service. More specialized—at least in this country—is Middle Eastern (Turkish) coffee that is brewed in an *ibrik*.

Drip coffee This popular method of brewing coffee can be done manually or automatically. In either case, hot water passes through coffee grounds that are held in a paper or wire mesh filter. The coffee drips into a carafe, ready to serve immediately.

French press   Also known as plunger pot coffee, this is an open-pot brewing method, meaning that the coffee grounds are put directly into a pot of water. In this case, the coffee is put into a narrow glass cylinder that is fitted with a fine mesh screen plunger. Hot water is poured into the pot and allowed to steep with the coffee grounds for about four minutes. The plunger is then slowly pushed, filtering the coffee as it carries the grounds to the bottom of the pot. This is a quite elegant way to serve coffee to guests at brunch or at a dinner party.

Ibrik   Turkish, or Middle Eastern, coffee can be made in any pot. However, to capture the sense of ritual and esthetics you will need an *ibrik*, as it is known in Turkey, or a *briki* from Greece. These small conical pots are made of copper or brass that is tinned inside. Coffee is ground to a powder-fine consistency and placed in the ibrik along with sugar and water. The coffee is then boiled and served in small demitasse cups with the grounds suspended in the sweet, heavy liquid.

Espresso machines   Coffee brewed in this manner requires more sophisticated equipment and is a bit more involved then

> I have measured out my life
> with coffee spoons.
> – *The Love Song of*
> *J. Alfred Prufrock*
> by T. S. Eliot

other methods. Hot water is forced under pressure through very finely ground, firmly packed coffee. A vast array of espresso makers are available at varying prices, but they fall into three basic categories.

- ❖ STOVE-TOP MAKERS. These are the least expensive, but they do have their drawbacks. Water is heated in the lower compartment to produce steam pressure that forces the water into the upper compartment through the grounds. It is difficult to control the water temperature and the amount of water that goes through the grounds. You often end up with a thin, overextracted and bitter brew. These machines are not equipped to froth milk.

- ❖ ELECTRIC STEAM MACHINES. These use steam pressure to force water through the grounds. Most machines of this type have no control over the flow of water through the brew head, thus the entire amount of water you put into the chamber will flow through. They have a steaming wand, but it is difficult to froth milk since the steam you need dissipates as the water drains through the brew head.

- ❖ PUMP OR PISTON MACHINES. To brew espresso drinks at home that will rival any good coffeehouse version, you need this type of machine. Both types heat the water to the correct temperature that is required for espresso—192 to

198 degrees F. The pump machines use an electric pump to force water through the grounds; the piston style relies on a hand-operated piston. Easy-to-use milk frothing wands are built in, and a switch activates a separate thermostat to heat the water to 250 to 270 degrees F—the necessary temperature for steaming and frothing milk. Their water reservoirs are large enough to hold adequate water and may be refilled while the machine is in use. I use a pump espresso machine and love the results.

Essential Tools for Making Chocolate and Cocoa Beverages

Cold and hot cocoa and chocolate drinks do not require specific equipment beyond the tools found in most kitchens. Measuring spoons and cups, a small heavy-bottomed sauce pan, a wire whisk, and possibly a thermometer, are all you need for hot beverages. Cold drinks require a blender.

> Simple pleasures . . . are the last refuge of the complex.
>
> –Oscar Wilde

Good coffee keeps more people
awake than a bad conscience.

—anonymous

4

BASIC TECHNIQUES FOR PREPARING COFFEE AND COCOA DRINKS

The beverages of coffee and espresso cuisine require basic techniques that, once mastered, will yield you delicious results at home.

Drip Coffee

Purchase freshly roasted beans, and if possible, grind them just before brewing. Select the correct grind for your drip system. Use 2 tablespoons of ground coffee (the equivalent to one standard measure) for every 6 ounces of cold water. At first, measure the amounts. Soon you will be able to eyeball it, automatically putting the correct quantity of beans in your grinder or filling your filter basket to the correct level.

Always use fresh water. Depending on the quality of your tap water, you may wish to use filtered or bottled water. The water should be just below boiling, 195 to 205 degrees F. Automatic drip brewers have a built-in thermostat to regulate the water temperature. If you are using a drip cone system, be sure to pour the measured amount of water through just before it comes to a boil—or if it boils, allow the water to cool a bit.

Drip coffee takes 4 to 6 minutes to brew with an automatic drip machine. It will take slightly longer with a drip cone system, as you must allow time for the water to reach a boil.

In 1793, a small group of auctioneers and merchants began meeting regularly at the Tontine Coffee House in New York City. Their enterprise eventually became the New York Stock Exchange.

Helpful Tips

The following tips will save you wastage and help you achieve a delicious pot of coffee every time.

✧ Unbleached paper coffee filters are more environmentally friendly than bleached white filters. Better yet, purchase a gold filter. They are made of a high-density plastic that is coated with 23-karat gold. To clean, simply discard the wet grounds and use a sponge and mild soap to wash the filter. Do not put it in the dishwasher as this will wear away the gold plating.

✧ Too fine a grind causes a bitter brew as the water is in contact with the surface area of the beans for too long a time. Too coarse a grind causes a watery coffee because the water passes through them too rapidly.

✧ Do not reuse coffee grounds. The delicious flavors are extracted in the initial brewing, leaving grounds that will yield a bitter brew the second time around.

✧ Too low a water temperature causes underextraction. The flavor compounds don't dissolve completely and the resulting coffee is weak. Too high a water temperature can actually burn the coffee, causing an unpleasant flavor.

- Brewed coffee retains its optimum freshness and full flavor for 20 to 30 minutes. Continuous heating on a coffee machine's heating plate causes the coffee to develop a sour and bitter taste.
- Thermal containers are the best way to hold coffee for extended periods of time. A temperature of 180 to 190 degrees F is optimum.
- Serve coffee in thin-walled china or glass cups. Thick-walled mugs, unless preheated, cause the coffee to cool down too quickly.

French Press and Open Pot Brewed Coffee

Open-pot brewing methods date back several centuries, and some of those traditions are still with us today. The most notable hail from the Middle East and Mexico. Unlike most coffee drinks that we are familiar with, this technique boils very finely ground coffee with water to produce a thick, rich brew.

French Press coffee (also known as plunger pot coffee) is an open-pot brewing method that steeps the coffee grounds in hot water. The grounds, which are coarser in this type of brewing, are forced to the bottom of the pot by pressing a fine mesh screen through the brew. The press method produces a rich flavorful brew, bringing out all of the qualities of the coffee as the grounds steep in the pot.

As with drip coffee, use 2 tablespoons of coffee per 6 ounces of water. Always use fresh water. Depending on the quality of your tap water, you may wish to use filtered or bottled water. The water should be just below boiling, 195 to 205 degrees F, so be sure to pour in the measured amount of water just before it comes to a boil—or if it boils, allow the water to cool a bit. Stir slightly, then place the plunger assembly loosely on the top to retain the heat. Steep for 4 minutes, then hold the pot by the handle and slowly press the plunger down through the liquid. The grounds will be carried to the bottom of the pot. Serve immediately.

Helpful Tips

These tips should help while you are learning to use your French press system.

✦ Preheat the pot and plunger assembly before adding the coffee and hot water.
✦ Do not overfill the pot with water—it will spill out of the spout when you depress the plunger assembly.
✦ Clean the pot and plunger with hot soapy water after each use.

Turkish or Middle Eastern Coffee

Since with this open-pot brewing method, you actually drink the coffee grounds, it is extremely important that you have very finely ground, almost powdery coffee. If you do not have a Middle Eastern coffee grinder as described earlier, purchase ground coffee packed in tins at specialty coffee retailers. The commercial grinder in some coffeehouses is also capable of achieving this fine grind, allowing you to have it fresh. Middle Eastern coffee is brewed from a fairly dark roast such as Italian. A blend of French roast and Sumatra is also nice.

Coffee, sugar, and water are all placed in a saucepan or ibrik to the half-full mark. As the coffee cooks for about 5 minutes, a foam builds up, filling the remaining space. The coffee is served immediately with the foam spooned on top.

Helpful Tips

When making Turkish or Middle Eastern coffee, these tips should prove helpful.

✧ Make sure your coffee is ground up to a powdery-fine consistency so you do not get grinds caught in your teeth or feel the need to remove them from your mouth.

- Leave plenty of room in the pot for the foam to build up as the coffee brews.
- Serve the coffee in small, preheated demitasse cups. Traditionally, it is served at the table, poured ceremoniously into each cup with the brown foam spooned on top.

Espresso Drinks

Preparing espresso is an art form unto itself. The steps are a ritual, each to be performed in a precise manner. Espresso, properly prepared, is not harsh but rather smooth and aromatic with a slight bitterness. *Crema,* the bittersweet creamy foam that tops an espresso, is the signature of a perfectly brewed cup. It occurs only when the right amount of fresh ground espresso beans have had the proper amount of water, at the precise temperature, forced through them by the steam of your espresso machine. Once the steps are mastered, you can brew the perfect cup every time.

The grind of the bean critical. A grind that feels like flour is too fine; it should be more like salt. Water cannot flow through a grind that is too fine, and if too coarse, it will flow so fast that the full body of the coffee will not be extracted and the crema will not be produced.

Once you get a mouthful of very hot coffee, whatever you do next is going to be wrong.

—anonymous

Preheat your espresso machine with the filter holder in the brew head. The time required will vary from machine to machine, so get to know how long it takes yours to reach the optimum temperature. This will take at least 5 minutes—longer than actually brewing a cup of espresso.

Remove the filter holder from the brew heat and insert the one- or two-serving metal basket. For the one cup basket, fill with about 1 tablespoon finely ground espresso coffee. Tamp the coffee lightly. You want to level the coffee, not tightly pack it. Wipe any grounds off of the edge of the filter holder since they will inhibit a tight seal on the brew head. Follow the same steps when using the two-cup basket, adding 2 tablespoons of grounds.

Insert the filter holder into the brew head and turn to lock it in place. If brewing one cup, place a warm espresso cup under the brew head, making sure that it is properly lined up. For two cups, place them side by side. Turn the machine on. After about 15 seconds, enough pressure will build up in the brew head and a trickle of dark espresso, followed by the golden crema, will flow into the cup. This will take between 18 and 25 seconds, depending on your machine. Turn off the switch as soon as 1 1/2 ounces—a shot of espresso— has been extracted.

Helpful Tips

Use the following tips to gain a mastery of your espresso maker.

- ❖ As with any coffee, depending on the quality of your tap water you may want to use filtered or bottled water.

- ❖ If the espresso does not come out of the brew head, several things could be wrong. First of all, check the obvious. Make sure there is water in the water reservoir and that the siphon hose is properly attached. Alternately, the coffee may be ground too finely, or tamped too hard, inhibiting the flow of water. Too many grounds in the filter basket could also be a problem.

- ❖ If the espresso comes out too quickly, the water in the machine may not have reached the proper temperature. Another cause is coffee that is ground too coarsely, or coffee that is stale. Too little coffee in the filter basket or not tamping the filter basket are other causes.

- ❖ Coffee spurting from where the filter holder is attached to the machine is an indication that it may not be properly locked in place or that the filter holder may not be making a proper seal due to grounds being in the way.

- ✦ If your espresso has a bitter taste, you may have allowed too much water to flow through the filter basket, thereby extracting the bitter oils from the grounds. Only allow 1 1/2 ounces of water to flow through the filter basket, per serving. If you do not like a strong espresso, simply dilute it with some hot water from the steam vent.

- ✦ If your espresso is not hot enough, you may not have allowed the machine to heat up long enough to bring the water to the proper brewing temperature, or you may not have preheated your cups.

- ✦ Use hot water to rinse the filter holder and metal coffee basket after each use. Several times a year you may wish to thoroughly clean them by soaking for several hours in a solution of 1 part white vinegar to 4 parts water. Baking soda is also recommended.

- ✦ Do not remove the brew head until the pressure has gone down. Failing to do so may result in a burn. Clean the brew head of your espresso machine after each use to prevent an oily residue buildup that will spoil the taste of your next espresso.

- ✦ Serve espresso in preheated 2- to 2 1/2-ounce demitasse cups, cappuccino in preheated 5-ounce cups, and café latté in 9-ounce cups.

Frothing Milk

Frothing—or steaming—milk is a process that heats milk and creates a head of froth, or foam. When poured atop hot espresso this not only keeps the coffee warm and provides a surface upon which to shake powdered cocoa or ground cinnamon, but also prevents a skin from forming on the surface of the milk as happens when milk is heated in a pan.

There are two foolproof, but completely different, techniques for frothing milk. One relies on a microwave oven, the other on an espresso machine with a frothing wand.

To froth milk in a *microwave oven,* pour the desired amount of cold milk into a deep, rather than shallow, bowl. Place the bowl in the microwave oven and heat it for 2 to 3 minutes, depending on the power level of your microwave. Remove it when scalded but not boiling. Using a hand crank mixer, lower the blades into the milk and rapidly crank until the milk is airy—frothed.

A pump-driven *expresso machine* will froth milk quickly and effortlessly once you become familiar with the process. These machines have a built-in thermostat to heat the water to one temperature to produce espresso, and another—slightly hotter—to produce the steam required to froth milk.

Each machine will give specific directions in the instructions manual; however, certain procedures are always the same.

Thoroughly preheat your machine. A "ready light" will go on or off, depending on the design. I allow mine an extra few minutes for good measure. Place a sponge or empty cup under the steam vent, then open the valve and allow any condensation to clear. This avoids watering down the milk. Close the valve once it's cleared.

Place the desired amount of cold milk in a chilled metal pitcher. Since quite a head of froth will build up, be sure that the pitcher is only one-third full.

Place the steam vent just below the surface of the milk, then open the steam valve completely. Keep the steam valve just below the surface of the milk, but do not allow it to reach the bottom of the pitcher. As the milk begins to froth, move the steam vent slightly up and down to incorporate more air as you foam. The milk will double in volume at which time you can further lower the steam valve to heat the remaining milk. Feel the bottom of the pitcher; it should be hot but not scalding.

Turn the steam vent off before removing the pitcher—otherwise, hot milk will splatter.

Helpful Tips

Frothing milk is an elegant touch surrounded by mystery. These tips will help make this process simple.

- Frothing pitchers are available in 10- to 20-ounce sizes. The larger size is necessary for steaming milk for a latté or steamed hot cocoa. Store yours in the freezer or refrigerator since very cold milk froths the best.

- Put cold milk in a cold frothing pitcher just before you are ready to steam it. Lower the tip of the frothing wand to just below the surface of the milk and open the valve.

- When the tip of the frothing wand is correctly placed in the milk, you will hear a hissing sound, the surface of the milk will begin to seethe, and small bubbles will begin to form. If the wand is lowered too deeply into the milk, it will sound more like a rumble, and large bubbles will form.

- Frothed milk should be smooth and thick with small bubbles. Large bubbles dissipate more quickly.

- Steamed milk should be present at the bottom of the pitcher; not all the milk will be transformed to froth. Overheating the milk will destroy the froth. Touch the bottom of the pitcher with your fingers; when it is hot, not scalding, the milk is steamed.

- Always froth the milk before heating it. Warm or stale milk will not froth. Lowfat milk will froth more easily because it contains less butterfat.

- ✦ Clean your frothing wand after every use. Open the steam vent for several seconds to force out any milk that may have entered. Then use a damp cloth to wipe the steam vent clean before the milk hardens on it.

- ✦ If you forget to clean your frothing wand and a milk residue hardens on it, immerse it in a tall glass of hot water overnight and wipe it clean in the morning. Before frothing milk, be sure to allow some steam to run through the wand to clean out any hardened milk.

Spain's Princess Maria Theresa made chocolate the rage of Europe when she presented cocoa beans as an engagement gift to Louis XIV.

Basic Techniques for Preparing Cocoa and Chocolate Beverages

Blending the cocoa powder with hot water to form a smooth paste is the most critical element to producing a quality hot or cold cocoa-based drink. For hot drinks, start with a clean sauce pan and stir together the cocoa powder and sugar. Whisk in hot water until a smooth paste has been achieved. Heat over medium heat as you whisk in cold milk. Do not allow the mixture to come to a boil—remove from the heat when small bubbles begin to form around the edges. Whisk again to froth slightly, then serve steaming hot.

Cold cocoa or chocolate drinks also rely on thoroughly blended ingredients. A high-quality blender is essential. The blender should not be filled to more than two-thirds of its capacity—you need plenty of head room for the foam to develop. These beverages taste best when served icy cold.

Helpful Tips

The following suggestions are presented to help you be an expert at service cocoa and chocolate beverages—whatever the temperature.

✧ Use Dutch process cocoa for hot or cold drinks. It has a slightly softer, more delicate flavor.

✧ Serve hot cocoa drinks in preheated 5-ounce mugs.

✧ Chill the blender bucket before preparing cold blended drinks.

✧ Serve cold cocoa drinks in chilled glasses. Old-fashioned soda fountain glasses are particularly fun.

In 1657, the first of many English "chocolate houses" were established to serve the drink to the general public.

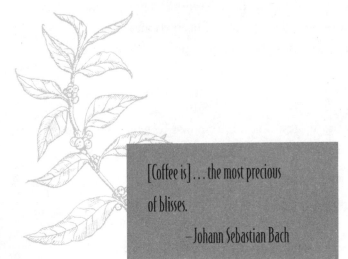

[Coffee is]…the most precious of blisses.

—Johann Sebastian Bach

5

FRESHLY BREWED COFFEE DRINKS

The comfort of your own home is the perfect place to enjoy coffee and espresso—alone or with family and friends. Every season presents the perfect setting. Enjoy a rainy day by the fire with a hot mug of Chocolate Raspberry Cappuccino in hand and a good book in your lap. In midsummer, when it is steaming hot outside, an Almond Espresso Spritzer will quench your thirst and lift your energy. Or linger over French Roast Coffee with Vanilla and Cream, enjoying conversation with friends.

Bring home and sample the vast array of coffees available at your local specialty coffee retailer. Stock your pantry with some flavored syrups, cocoas, and extracts, then experiment with the recipes I present here. Have fun creating your own.

Hot Brewed Coffee Drinks

Many coffee brewing machines are available for home use, exhibiting a wide range of methods and styles. They all achieve the same end—separating the grounds from the coffee as it is brewed. Either manual or electric, coffee brewed by this method requires precise measurement and water temperature.

The standard serving size for a cup of brewed coffee is 6 ounces. To achieve this, start with 1 scoop—equal to 2 tablespoons—of ground coffee for each 6 ounces of cold water.

Water, heated to just below boiling, then passes through the grounds, extracting the rich flavor. See page 47 for helpful tips.

French Roast Coffee with Vanilla and Cream

This dark French roast coffee is delicious with Chocolate Espresso Cake (see page 118).

SERVES 4

¹/₂ cup ground French roast coffee
3 cups cold water
¹/₄ cup vanilla syrup
3 tablespoons half-and-half

Place the coffee grounds in a filter basket. Brew the coffee by manual or automatic drip method. Stir the vanilla syrup and half-and-half into the brewed coffee and serve in warm cups.

Coconut Kona Coffee

SERVES 4

¹/₂ cup ground Kona coffee
3 cups cold water
¹/₄ cup coconut syrup

Place the coffee grounds in a filter basket. Brew the coffee by manual or automatic drip method. Stir the coconut syrup and serve in warm cups.

Fruit- and nut-flavored syrups are used in many recipes throughout this book. These presweetened extracts are available in many coffee shops and specialty markets. Popular brands are Torani and Monin.

63

Brewed Coffee with Cinnamon and Nutmeg

This coffee is best made with a medium-bodied coffee. The cinnamon and nutmeg are very aromatic, filling the kitchen with a wonderful scent as the coffee brews.

SERVES 4

$^1/_2$ cup ground medium-bodied coffee
$^1/_4$ teaspoon ground cinnamon
Scant $^1/_8$ teaspoon freshly ground nutmeg
3 cups cold water

Place the coffee grounds in a filter basket and sprinkle the cinnamon and nutmeg on top. Brew the coffee by manual or automatic drip method. Serve immediately in warm cups.

Coffee Masala

The light acidity and slight chocolate aftertaste make Mocha beans the perfect choice for this popular Indian style coffee.

SERVES 4

$^1/_2$ cup ground Mocha coffee
3 cups cold water
$^1/_8$ teaspoon ground cardamom
Several grinds nutmeg

Place the coffee grounds in a filter basket and top them with the cardamom and nutmeg. Brew the coffee by manual or automatic drip method. Serve immediately in warm cups.

Iced Brewed Coffee Drinks

Iced coffee drinks are one of the many pleasures of summer. Drip brewed coffee may be prepared early in the day and chilled for afternoon enjoyment. Coffee brewed by the French Press method (pages 48–49) can form the base for an instant indulgence.

The Iced Coffee with Chocolate Menthe, Raspberry Iced Coffee, and Orgeat Iced Coffee recipes can easily be increased to serve and delight afternoon guests or to add a lift to picnic basket fare.

Iced Coffee with Chocolate Menthe

Chocolate menthe is a nonalcoholic extract sold in many specialty food stores. This iced coffee drink is especially good on a hot summer day when you need a delicious afternoon lift. Use a medium roast coffee, such as Ethiopia Sidamo or Kona.

SERVES 2

1 1/2 cups brewed coffee, chilled
1/2 teaspoon chocolate menthe
4 teaspoons half-and-half
2 sprigs fresh mint

Combine the coffee, chocolate menthe, and half-and-half. Put several cubes of ice into 10-ounce glasses and pour the coffee over the ice. Garnish with the mint sprig. Serve immediately.

Raspberry Iced Coffee

Use a medium-bodied coffee such as Colombia Supremo or Guatemala Antigua for this invigorating drink.

SERVES 2

1 ¹/₂ cups brewed coffee, chilled
2 tablespoons raspberry syrup
¹/₂ cup lowfat milk
2 fresh mint sprigs

Combine the coffee, raspberry syrup, and milk. Put several cubes of ice into two 10-ounce glasses and pour the coffee over the ice. Garnish with the mint sprig. Serve immediately.

Orgeat Iced Coffee

The richness of the half-and-half complements the nutty almond flavor of this bracing iced coffee.

SERVES

1 ¹/₂ cups brewed coffee, chilled
2 teaspoons orgeat syrup
2 teaspoons half-and-half
2 fresh mint sprigs

Combine the coffee, orgeat syrup, and half-and-half. Put several cubes of ice into two 10-ounce glasses and pour the coffee over the ice. Garnish with the mint sprig. Serve immediately.

Orgeat is almond-flavored syrup, a preparation extracted from barley and almonds.

French Roast Ice Cream Float

I enjoy this float for lunch on a hot day. You may use any dark roast coffee—my favorite is French roast. Make sure that you chill the glasses.

SERVES 2

1 1/2 cups brewed French roast coffee, chilled
1 cup cold club soda
2 tablespoons granulated sugar
2 large scoops vanilla ice cream
Powdered cocoa

Combine the coffee, club soda, and sugar in a container and briefly set aside. Put a scoop of ice cream in each chilled 12-ounce glass, then pour in the coffee mixture. Dust with powdered cocoa. Serve immediately with a straw and long-handled spoon.

Kona Freeze

SERVES 2

1 1/2 cups brewed Kona coffee, chilled
2 tablespoons coconut syrup
1/2 cup cold lowfat milk
1 cup crushed ice

Place the coffee, coconut syrup, and milk in a blender. Add the ice, cover and blend for about 30 seconds. Pour into chilled 10-ounce glasses. Serve immediately.

Hot French Press and Open Pot Coffees

French press coffeemakers are quite the rage today. They brew an excellent coffee with bit of fine sediment that gives the coffee a thick, full bodied flavor. Remember to use coarse grounds for French Press (plunger pot) coffees, so that the sediment is filtered out. When making Middle Eastern open-pot coffees, use a finer grind because the sediment is ingested with the blend.

I recommend preheating the pot and the cups when you are serving hot French Press coffee. When brewing coffee by this method for cold beverages you need not preheat the pot.

French Press Coffee with Cardamom and Ginger

Press coffee most commonly uses a dark roast coffee; however, your favorite selection will produce a flavorful brew.

SERVES 4

1/2 cup coarse ground dark roast coffee
1/8 teaspoon ground cardamom
Pinch ground ginger
3 cups hot water

Bring the water to a boil, remove from the heat and allow to cool slightly. Place the coffee, cardamom, and ginger in the pot of a plunger press. Pour in the water and place the plunger assembly on the top, but do not push down on the plunger. Allow to steep for 4 minutes, then slowly press down on the plunger. This will carry the coffee grounds to the bottom of the pot. Serve immediately with sugar, if you wish.

Traditional Middle Eastern Coffee

Dark roast coffee is traditionally used for Middle Eastern—also known as Turkish—coffee. Have your coffee retailer finely grind Italian roast for you. For a variation, add a pinch of cardamom to the pot along with the sugar.

SERVES 2

4 teaspoons finely ground dark roast coffee
2 teaspoons sugar
¹/₄ cup cold water

Place the coffee and sugar in a small saucepan, or in a traditional ibrik. Add the water and heat over medium-high. After a few minutes the coffee will begin to gently boil. A darkish crust will form on the top of the foam as it works its way up the sides of the saucepan or ibrik. Watch closely—you do not want the pot to overflow. Serve in demitasse cups, taking care that the foam does not settle.

Sweetening one's coffee is generally the first stirring event of the day.

—anonymous

Café de Olla

This is a traditional Mexican coffee drink and is usually prepared in a clay pot. All of the ingredients go directly in the pot and simmer to marry the flavors. If you can find panocha (piloncillo), the cone shaped brown sugar from Mexico, use 4 small cones in place of the brown sugar.

SERVES 4

4 cups cold water
1/2 cup coarsely ground Viennese roast coffee
1/2 cup dark brown sugar
1 4-inch cinnamon stick
4 whole cloves
Peel from 1/2 of an orange, sliced

Place the water in a small sauce pan over high heat and bring it to a boil. Reduce heat slightly and add the coffee, sugar, cinnamon stick, cloves, and orange peel. Gently simmer for 5 minutes, then stir in 1/2 cup cold water. Strain through a paper coffee filter into a warm pot. Serve immediately in warm clay mugs.

Iced French Press Coffee

Any flavorful beans may be used for iced coffee. Since plunger-pot brewers and the process of icing coffee highlight the coffee beans' brightest flavors, try beans such as Ethiopia Sidamo, Kenya, or Sumatra.

Basic Iced French Press Coffee

Enjoy this instant iced coffee black, or use it as the base-coffee for other iced coffee recipes in this book.

SERVES 6

1 cup coarsely ground Ethiopia Sidamo coffee
3 cups hot water

Bring the water to a boil, remove from the heat and allow to cool slightly. Place the coffee in the pot of a plunger press. Pour in the water and place the plunger assembly on the top, but do not push down on the plunger. Allow to steep for 4 minutes, then slowly press down on the plunger. This will carry the coffee grounds to the bottom of the pot. Fill a pitcher with ice cubes and pour the coffee directly over the ice cubes. Serve immediately with sugar, if you wish.

Hot Espresso Drinks

Espresso has been popular in Europe since the early 1900s, but has just won the hearts of Americans within the last 20 years. Today excellent home brewing espresso machines are available, bringing this invigorating beverage directly into our kitchens. See the general tips for brewing espresso and frothing milk in chapter 4. Since each machine is slightly different, be sure to consult your instruct manual.

Italian Espresso

In Italy, espresso is most often served in its pure form. I fell in love with it this way while wandering through the inner city of Venice. In Rome and in America, it is frequently served with a lemon zest.

SERVES 2

2 shots espresso
1 teaspoon granulated sugar

Brew the espresso and place it in small, warm espresso cups. Serve, then stir 1/2 teaspoon sugar into each cup.

Orgeat Cappuccino

This almond-flavored syrup is delightful when added to cappuccino, producing a delicious after-dinner beverage. I also enjoy it as a mid-afternoon treat.

SERVES 2

2 shots espresso
2 teaspoons orgeat syrup
1/2 cup cold lowfat milk

Brew the espresso and place it in warm 5-ounce cups. Stir 1 teaspoon orgeat syrup into each cup and briefly set aside. Place the cold milk in a cold frothing pitcher and steam. Pour in equal amounts of steamed milk into each cup. Spoon the froth on top. Serve immediately.

Yule Latté

When the holiday season rolls around, we all think of eggnog. Here, Londa Wagner has devised a way to combine it with another favorite winter beverage—a latté.

SERVES 2

2 shots espresso
1 1/2 cups eggnog
2 tablespoons powdered white chocolate
2 teaspoons hazelnut syrup
Powdered cinnamon
Freshly grated nutmeg

Brew the espresso and briefly set it aside. Place the eggnog in a cold frothing pitcher and steam. Since eggnog is so rich, you will not get a lot of froth, but some will develop as you heat it through. Place 1 tablespoon white chocolate and 1 teaspoon hazelnut syrup in the bottom of each warm mug and pour in equal amounts of steamed eggnog. Stir to dissolve the chocolate and syrup. Place a long-handled spoon in each warm mug, then cap off with a bit of froth. Pour a shot of espresso down the center of each mug. Dust with cinnamon and nutmeg and serve immediately.

Caramel Hazelnut Cappuccino

This is coffee and dessert all in one. The nutty aroma, rich coffee flavor and caramel sweetness is heaven in a cup.

SERVES 2

2 shots espresso
2 teaspoons caramel syrup
1/2 cup cold lowfat milk
1 tablespoon hazelnut syrup

Brew the espresso and place it in warm 5-ounce cups. Stir 1 teaspoon caramel syrup into each cup. Place the milk in a cold frothing pitcher and add the hazelnut syrup. Steam, then pour equal amounts of steamed milk mixture into each cup. Spoon the froth on top and serve immediately.

Chocolate Raspberry Cappuccino

Berries and chocolate are a delightful combination. When you add them to a cappuccino, the results are delicious.

SERVES 2

2 shots espresso
2 teaspoons chocolate syrup
2 teaspoons raspberry syrup
1/2 cup cold lowfat milk

Brew the espresso and place it in warm 5-ounce cups. Stir in the chocolate syrup and raspberry syrup. Place the milk in a cold frothing pitcher and steam. Pour equal amounts of steamed milk mixture over the espresso, and spoon the froth on top. Serve immediately.

Honey Streaked Latté

Rush Haven, a coffee shop in Fair Oaks, California, prepares this latté calling it Café Miel. The beverage is free-form art in a glass—the honey streaks down the sides of the mug creating unique patterns. Be sure to serve it in a clear mug for the full effect.

SERVES 2

2 shots espresso
1 1/2 cup cold lowfat milk
4 teaspoons honey, plus several drops

Brew the espresso and briefly set it aside. Place the milk in a cold frothing pitcher and steam. Place 2 teaspoons honey in the bottom of each mug and pour in equal amounts of steamed milk. Stir to dissolve the honey. Place a long-handled spoon in each warm mug, then cap off with a bit of froth. Pour a shot of espresso down the center of each mug. Place several drops of honey around the outer edges and serve immediately.

The pedigree of honey
Does not concern the bee;
A clover, any time, to him
Is aristocracy.

—Emily Dickinson

Coconut Café Mocha

This mocha reminds me of German chocolate cake.

SERVES 2

2 shots espresso
1 1/2 cups cold lowfat milk
2 tablespoons Dutch process cocoa
2 tablespoons coconut syrup

Brew the espresso and briefly set it aside. Place the milk in a cold frothing pitcher and steam. Place 1 tablespoon of the cocoa and 1 tablespoon coconut syrup in the bottom of each warm mug and pour in equal amounts of steamed milk. Stir to dissolve the cocoa. Place a long-handled spoon in each mug, then cap off with a bit of froth. Pour a shot of espresso down the center of each mug. Serve immediately.

Café Americano

Café Americano is a good shot of espresso that has hot water added to it after it is brewed—not an espresso that has had more water forced though the grounds. The flavor is rich and delicious.

SERVES 2

2 shots espresso
1 cup hot water

Brew the espresso and put a shot in each warm 6-ounce mug. Add 1/2 cup of hot water to each and stir to incorporate. Serve immediately.

Sweet Mexican Mocha

This beverage is a wonderful way to begin the day. You will actually look forward to the alarm clock's ring.

SERVES 2

2 shots espresso
1 1/2 cups cold lowfat milk
2 tablespoons Dutch process cocoa
2 tablespoons Mexican powdered chocolate
2 teaspoons honey

Brew the espresso and briefly set it aside. Place the milk in a cold frothing pitcher and steam. Place 1 tablespoon of the cocoa and chocolate in the bottom of each warm mug and pour in equal amounts of steamed milk. Add 1 teaspoon of honey to each mug and stir to dissolve. Place a long-handled spoon in each mug, then cap off with a bit of froth. Pour a shot of espresso down the center of each mug. Serve immediately.

Even if a farmer intends to loaf, he gets up in time to get an early start.

—Edgar Watson Howe

Iced Espresso Drinks

Iced espresso drinks are a quenching summer beverage. The possibilities are almost endless. Some are served over ice, others whirled in the blender with crushed ice to quickly create a cool beverage. Chill your glasses, sit back and enjoy.

Cinnamon Cappuccino Slush

This slush will take you back to your childhood days. Extremely refreshing, it can be served any time the temperature soars and guests drop by.

SERVES 2

2 cups lowfat milk
2 shots espresso
2 teaspoons sugar
1/4 teaspoon ground cinnamon

Place the milk in an ice cube tray and freeze for several hours until solid. If you are doing this in advance, cover the tray. The frozen cubes may be used over the course of about a week.

Brew two shot of espresso and briefly set them aside. Place the milk cubes in a blender and add the espresso, sugar, and cinnamon. Pulse to process until smooth, about a minute. If necessary scrape down the sides in-between pulses. Pour into chilled 10-ounce glasses and garnish with mint sprigs if desired. Serve immediately with a spoon.

Iced Chocolate Malted Cappuccino

Dessert and coffee all in one! Serve this bitter-sweet beverage to finish a summer dinner. If you have fresh mint in your garden, garnish each glass with a mint sprig.

SERVES 2

2 shots espresso
$1/2$ cup lowfat milk
1 teaspoon malted milk powder
2 teaspoons sugar
2 teaspoons Dutch process cocoa
$1 1/2$ cup crushed ice

Brew two shots of espresso and briefly set them aside. Place the milk, malted milk powder, sugar, and cocoa powder in a blender and add the crushed ice. Pour in the espresso. Cover and blend for about 30 seconds until frothy. Pour into two chilled 10-ounce glasses. Serve immediately.

Iced Espresso Romano

Simple and refreshing, this drink is just the ticket when you want a jolt of energy on a hot day.

SERVES 2

2 shots espresso
2 teaspoon granulated sugar
2 half-inch pieces lemon peel
1 cup crushed ice

Brew two shots of espresso and add 1 teaspoon of sugar to each, stirring to dissolve. Place 1/2 cup of crushed ice into each chilled 8-ounce glass. Pour equal amounts of the espresso into each glass over the ice. Garnish each with lemon peel. Serve immediately.

Almond Espresso Spritzer

This is a most refreshing coffee beverage. The orgeat syrup adds a hint of sweetness, and the club soda a delightful effervescence.

SERVES 2

2 shots espresso
2 tablespoons orgeat syrup
ice cubes
1 cup cold club soda

Brew two shots of espresso and mix 1 tablespoon orgeat syrup into each. Place 5 to 6 ice cubes in each chilled 12-ounce glass and pour the espresso over. Add the club soda; it will fizz and form a foam on the top. Serve with straws.

Mocha Mint Shake

A trip to the soda fountain was never as good as this. I have collected several old-fashioned milkshake glasses over the years and enjoy serving this shake in them.

SERVES 2

2 shots espresso
2 cups crushed ice
2 cups chocolate ice cream
1/2 cup lowfat milk
2 tablespoons creme de menthe syrup
2 sprigs fresh mint

Brew two shots of espresso and briefly set aside. Put the crushed ice in a blender and add the ice cream, milk, and creme de menthe syrup. Pour in the espresso and process until smooth, about one minute. Pour into two chilled 12-ounce glasses and garnish with the mint sprigs. Serve with straws and long-handled spoons.

In a recent Gallup poll, chocolate outscored any other flavor by a whopping 3 to 1 margin. In fact, 90 percent of all Americans consume some form of chocolate every day.
–Chocolate Manufacturers Association of the U.S.A.

Iced Cappuccino

This cappuccino is the perfect beverage to enjoy on a hot summer morning.

SERVES 2

2 shots espresso
1/2 cup lowfat milk
2 teaspoons granulated sugar
1 1/2 cups crushed ice
Cocoa powder

Coffee is a stimulant; if you drink it at breakfast, it will keep you awake all day.

Brew two shots of espresso and briefly set them aside. Place the milk and sugar in a blender and add the crushed ice. Pour in the espresso. Cover and blend for about 30 seconds until frothy. Pour into two chilled 10-ounce glasses. Sprinkle with the cocoa and serve.

Iced Caramel Cappuccino

Smooth and creamy, this cappuccino is a delightful afternoon treat.

SERVES 2

2 shots espresso
1/2 cup lowfat milk
1/4 cup caramel syrup
2 teaspoons granulated sugar
1 1/2 cup crushed ice

Brew two shots espresso and briefly set them aside. Place the milk, caramel syrup, and sugar in a blender and add the crushed ice. Pour in the espresso. Cover and blend for about 30 seconds until frothy. Pour into 2 chilled 10-ounce glasses. Serve immediately

Iced Raspberry White Chocolate Mocha

This pink drink takes me back to being a little girl. It looks like the strawberry shakes my mother used to make during the summertime for dessert.

SERVES 2

2 shots espresso
2 tablespoon powdered white chocolate
2 tablespoons raspberry syrup
1 cup cold lowfat milk
2 cups crushed ice
whipped cream, optional

Brew two shots of espresso and briefly set aside. Put the white chocolate, raspberry syrup, and milk in a blender and add the crushed ice. Pour in the espresso. Cover and blend for about 40 seconds until frothy. Pour into two chilled 12-ounce glasses. Top with whip cream, if desired, and serve immediately.

Iced Caramel Mocha

The Mexican chocolate lends a slightly spicy flavor to this refreshing iced mocha. The chocolate is available in specialty coffeehouses and markets.

SERVES 2

2 shots espresso
2 tablespoons powdered Mexican chocolate
2 teaspoons caramel syrup
1 cup cold lowfat milk
2 cups crushed ice

Brew two shots of espresso and briefly set aside. Put the chocolate, caramel syrup and milk in a blender and add the crushed ice. Pour in the espresso. Cover and blend for about 40 seconds until frothy. Pour into two chilled 12-ounce glasses. Serve immediately.

Vanilla Hazelnut Spritzer

The hazelnut gives this spritzer a nutty aroma while the vanilla yields a richness. You might garnish it with a lemon wedge.

SERVES 2

2 shots espresso
2 tablespoons vanilla syrup
2 teaspoons hazelnut syrup
ice cubes
1 cup cold club soda

Brew two shots of espresso and mix 1 tablespoon vanilla and 1 teaspoon hazelnut syrup into each shot. Place 5 to 6 ice cubes into two chilled 12-ounce glasses and pour the espresso over. Add the club soda, it will fizz and form a foam on the top. Serve with straws.

Coffee with Spirits

The easiest way to measure a shot of alcohol is with a shot glass—roughly equal to 1 tablespoon. If you do not have one, just use a standard tablespoon measure.

I recommend dark roast coffee as the base for these drinks. The liquor flavor has its own intensity and needs the bracing strength of a dark roast brew.

Coffee with Brandy

A very dark roast coffee is best for this after-dinner drink. Use Italian or French roast.

SERVES 2

2 teaspoons granulated sugar
1 1/2 cups brewed French roast coffee
2 shots brandy

Place 1 teaspoon of sugar in the bottom of each warm cup and add the coffee. Gently pour in brandy and serve immediately.

Irish Coffee

A dark roast is usually used for Irish coffee, but always choose a good Irish or Scotch whiskey.

SERVES 2

2 teaspoons granulated sugar
1 1/2 cups brewed Viennese coffee
2 shots Irish whiskey
1/4 cup lightly whipped cream

Place 1 teaspoon of sugar in the bottom of each warm cup and add the coffee. Gently pour in the whiskey, allowing it to float on the top. Spoon equal amounts of the whipped cream over the top and serve. The coffee is not stirred, but rather sipped through the layer of cream.

Kahlua Cream Soda

This refreshing Kahlua drink is a lovely way to end a summertime dinner.

SERVES 4

1/2 cup cold lowfat milk
1/2 cup Kahlua
1 1/2 cups cold club soda

Place crushed ice in four chilled 8-ounce glasses. Add equal amounts of the milk, Kahlua, and club soda to each glass. Stir well and serve immediately.

Homemade Kahlua

Homemade Kahlua is quite easy to make, and is a wonderful gift to give during the holiday season. Prepare it several months in advance, and put it in attractive bottles.

MAKES 6 CUPS

2 ounces powdered espresso
4 cups sugar
2 cups vodka
2 whole vanilla beans

Bring 2 cups of water to a boil. Remove from the heat and whisk in the espresso powder and sugar until completely dissolved. Set aside to cool. Whisk several times while it is cooling so the sugar does not settle on the bottom.

Add the vodka and stir very well to blend, then transfer to a bottle that has a tight-fitting lid. Slice the vanilla beans lengthwise and place them in the bottle. Secure the lid. Allow to set for about a month in a cool, dark place. Decant into smaller bottles, removing the vanilla bean. Enjoy a shot mixed into coffee, or by itself over ice.

Canadian Coffee

My fellow Soroptimist, Julita Fong, shares this recipe. She and her late husband took a trip across Canada several years ago, sampling coffee drinks as they went. This was their favorite, and Julita says it is guaranteed to warm you inside-out.

SERVES 2

2 shots Kahlua
2 shots Amaretto
2 shots Bailey's Irish Cream
1 1/2 cups dark roast coffee
1/4 cup whipped cream

Place one shot of Kahlua, Amaretto, and Bailey's Irish Cream in each warm mug. Add the coffee and top with whipped cream. Serve immediately.

Coffee affords a good restoring draught.

—Delille

6

SOOTHING COCOA AND CHOCOLATE DRINKS

Cocoa and chocolate drinks are loved by young and old alike. They are quick and easy to prepare any time of the year. Snuggle in bed on a cold night with a mug of Orange Spice Hot Chocolate. Serve Milk Frothed with Chocolate and Mint for a summertime dessert. Indulge in a Double Chocolate Almond Shake in your backyard on a hot afternoon.

Special equipment is not required for most cocoa and chocolate drinks. They do, however, need good quality cocoa and chocolate to achieve the richest flavor. Make sure that both are fresh, and keep plenty of cold milk on hand. Flavored syrups and malt open up an array of possibilities—keep them in your pantry.

Enjoy these recipes—no special occasion is necessary. Delight also in recreating some of your childhood favorites.

Hot Chocolate Drinks

All you need for most hot chocolate drinks is a heat source, a sauce pan, and a mug. Add the cocoa and milk and you are ready for instant pleasure. On a camping trip or in your home, these drinks are delicious.

Orange Spice Hot Chocolate

The orange extract gives this hot chocolate a wonderful flavor. Serve garnished with fresh orange wedges, if desired.

SERVES 2

2 tablespoons Dutch process cocoa
2 tablespoons granulated sugar
$^1/_8$ teaspoon ground cinnamon
Pinch freshly ground nutmeg
pinch salt
$^1/_4$ teaspoon orange extract
$^1/_4$ cup hot water
1 $^1/_2$ cup lowfat milk
2 orange wedges

Place cocoa, sugar, cinnamon, nutmeg, and salt in a sauce pan. Gradually whisk in the orange extract and hot water. Heat over medium-high to a rapid simmer and cook for 2 minutes, stirring constantly. Gradually pour in the milk, whisking to incorporate, and heat through but do not boil. Remove from the heat and beat with a hand-crank beater until slightly foamy, about a minute. Serve immediately.

Thomas Jefferson, an acknowledged gourmand, extolled chocolate's virtues, describing "the superiority of chocolate for both health and nourishment."

Steamed Hot Chocolate

This is coffeehouse-style hot chocolate, but simple to make at home if you have an espresso machine.

SERVES 2

2 tablespoons Dutch process cocoa
2 teaspoons granulated sugar
2 cups cold lowfat milk
1/4 to 1/2 cup whipped cream

Place 1 tablespoon of the cocoa and 1 teaspoon of the sugar in the bottom of each warm mug. Steam the milk with an espresso machine according to the directions beginning on page 54. Pour about 1/4 cup hot milk into each cup and stir to dissolve the cocoa. Fill the cups with the remaining milk and stir again. Top with the froth or the desired amount of whipped cream. Dust with additional cocoa and serve immediately.

Mexican Hot Chocolate

The Mexican chocolate and honey give this hot chocolate a luscious flavor.

SERVES 2

2 tablespoons powdered Mexican chocolate
2 tablespoons honey
1/4 cup hot water
1 1/2 cup lowfat milk

Place chocolate, honey, and hot water in a sauce pan and whisk to combine. Heat over medium-high to a rapid simmer and cook for 2 minutes, stirring constantly. Gradually pour in the milk, whisking to incorporate, and heat through but do not boil. Remove from the heat and beat with a hand-crank beater until slightly foamy, about a minute. Serve immediately.

Classic Hot Cocoa

Once you taste, or re-taste, the goodness of "from scratch" hot cocoa it will be hard to go back to the instant variety. This does take a few extra minutes but the resulting beverage is worth the time. Top with whipped cream, if desired.

SERVES 2

2 tablespoons Dutch process cocoa
2 tablespoons granulated sugar
pinch salt
1/4 cup hot water
1 1/2 cup lowfat milk

Place cocoa, sugar, and salt in a sauce pan and gradually whisk in the hot water. Heat over medium-high to a rapid simmer and cook for 2 minutes, stirring constantly. Gradually pour in the milk whisking to incorporate, and heat through but do not boil. Remove from the heat and beat with a hand-crank beater until slightly foamy, about a minute. Serve immediately.

Cold Chocolate Drinks

I enjoy these drinks for breakfast on a hot day. What a pleasurable way to get that necessary calcium! All that you need is a blender and a tall chilled glass. Children love these drinks as an after-school treat or for a summertime dessert.

Chocolate Malted Milk

Malted milk drinks were popular in the 1950's and 1960's, and this one tastes just as good today.

SERVES 2

2 cups cold lowfat milk
$1/3$ cup chocolate syrup
$1/4$ cup malted milk powder

Place the milk in a blender and add the chocolate syrup, malted milk powder, and $2/3$ cup crushed ice. Cover and blend until smooth. Serve in two chilled 10-ounce glasses.

Chocolate Milk with Raspberry Syrup

You don't have to be a child to enjoy this chocolate milk. I enjoy it as a refreshing afternoon beverage. It is a great way to use up the last bit of cold coffee from the morning pot.

SERVES 2

Chocolate played a part in the nourishment of the Allied Armed Forces during World War II. Even today, U.S. Army D-rations include three 4-ounce chocolate bars. Chocolate has also been transported into space as part of the diet of the U.S. astronauts.

1 cup lowfat milk
1 cup brewed coffee, chilled
2 tablespoons chocolate syrup
1 teaspoon raspberry syrup

Place the milk, coffee, chocolate syrup, and raspberry syrup in the blender. Blend for about 30 seconds to combine. Place several ice cubes in two chilled 12-ounce glasses and pour the milk over them. Serve immediately.

Milk Frothed with Chocolate and Mint

My nieces, Lindsey and Natalie, like this just as much as chocolate mint ice cream. It is especially refreshing for dessert on a hot day. For a variation, substitute 2 tablespoons raspberry syrup for the mint syrup.

SERVES 2

2 cups cold lowfat milk
2 tablespoons chocolate syrup
2 tablespoons mint syrup
1 cup crushed ice

Place the milk, chocolate syrup, and mint syrup in the blender. Add the crushed ice and blend for about 1 minute until frothy. Pour into chilled 12-ounce glasses. The milk will settle to the bottom creating a layer of froth on the top. Garnish with fresh mint, if desired.

Chocolate is "The Food of the Gods."

—Linnaeus

Double Chocolate Almond Shake

Chocolate and orgeat syrup are a marriage made in heaven. Indulge in this dreamy shake whenever you dare.

SERVES 2

2 large scoops chocolate ice cream
3/4 cup cold milk
2 tablespoons chocolate syrup
1 tablespoon orgeat syrup

Place the ice cream, milk, chocolate syrup, orgeat syrup, and 3/4 cup crushed ice in the blender. Blend until smooth, about a minute. Pour into chilled 10-ounce glasses and serve with straws and long-handled spoons.

Iced Mexican Chocolate with Kahlua

You may use the Homemade Kahlua (page 87) or purchase it already made.

SERVES 2

1 1/2 cups lowfat milk
2 tablespoons powdered Mexican chocolate
2 shots Kahlua

Place the milk, Mexican chocolate, and Kahlua in the blender. Blend for about 30 seconds until smooth. Serve over ice in chilled 10-ounce glasses.

This drink is also good hot. Whisk together $1/4$ cup of the milk with the powdered chocolate in a small sauce pan. Heat over medium, then whisk in the remaining milk. Put the Kahlua in warm mugs and add the milk. This is a great mid-winter bedtime drink.

Chocolate Syrup

In a sauce pan, combine 1 cup Dutch process cocoa and $3/4$ cup granulated sugar. Whisk in $3/4$ cup water and $1/2$ cup light corn syrup. Bring to a boil over medium-heat, stirring constantly. Remove from the heat, then stir in 1 teaspoon vanilla extract. Cool, transfer to a jar, and refrigerate.

I'd make a thousand trips
To his Lips,
If I were a bee,
Because he's sweeter than
Chocolate candy to me ...
he's confectionery.

—Billie Holiday

98

7

TASTY TREATS FROM THE OVEN

Friends gathering at home for morning coffee and coffee cake may be a thing of the past, but the tradition is well worth reviving, even if just on weekends. Baked goodies, hot from the oven, evoke a coziness that is enjoyed by all.

A Word about Baking with Chocolate

Melting chocolate is tricky. It can burn easily in a microwave oven or a double broiler. Whatever method you use, go slowly—you want to melt the chocolate, not cook it. Dark chocolate should not be heated above 120 degrees F, and milk or white chocolate should be kept just below 110 degrees F. If overheated, chocolate becomes gritty and develops a bad taste.

The following substitutions may be made:

1 ounce unsweetened chocolate	=	3 tablespoons cocoa powder + 1 tablespoon oil
1 ounce semisweet chocolate	=	3 tablespoons cocoa powder + 1 tablespoon oil + 1 tablespoon granulated sugar

Do not substitute sweetened cocoas or hot chocolate mixes for cocoa powder!

Helpful Tips for Baking

Once you get used to some of the tips provided below, they will become a welcome part of your culinary skills.

- Set out refrigerated ingredients such as eggs and butter an hour or two before you begin recipes so they have time to come to room temperature. Set dry ingredients on the counter as well so that you have everything on hand.

- Be sure to preheat the oven for at least 15 minutes. Use an oven thermometer to verify that the correct temperature has been reached before baking.

- Luckily, most baked goods freeze well, so they may be made when time permits and warmed in the oven for instant enjoyment. Coffee cakes should be cooked as directed and allowed to cool completely on a rack, then sliced or frozen whole. Wrap them tightly in a freezer bag. When ready to serve, remove them from the freezer and place directly in a preheated 325-degree F oven. Bake for 10 to 30 minutes, depending on the size of the slice or cake. Scones should also be baked, then completely cooled before being placed in freezer bags. Put frozen scones on a baking sheet and heat in a preheated 325-degree oven for 10 minutes.

- Sifting together the flour and baking powder or soda is a necessary step in some recipes.
- Invest in good heavy baking sheets and pans. They will not warp in the oven and will last you a lifetime.
- Wooden spoons and glass bowls are the best choices to use when mixing batter. Some recipes require an electric mixer.
- Remove baked goods from the oven to a cooling rack and allow to cool as indicated in the recipe before removing them from the pan or cookie sheet.

Blueberry Spice Coffee Cake

This coffee cake is inspired by a recipe that first appeared in Fast and Natural Cuisine, a cookbook co-authored with my longtime friend, Mindy Toomay. The delicate use of the strong spices complements the sweetness of the dried blueberries. Try it with dried cranberries or currents for a variation.

YIELD: 16 SERVINGS

The cake:
2 1/3 cups whole wheat pastry flour
1 teaspoon salt
2 teaspoons baking powder
1 teaspoon cinnamon
1/2 teaspoon nutmeg
2/3 cup unsalted butter

³/₄ cup honey
1 cup buttermilk
3 large eggs
¹/₄ cup dried blueberries

The topping:
1 tablespoon unsalted butter
¹/₄ cup honey
2 tablespoons buttermilk
¹/₄ teaspoon ground cinnamon
¹/₄ cup finely chopped walnuts

Preheat the oven to 350 degrees F. Lightly butter a 8 × 8 × 2-inch cake pan. In a medium bowl, sift together the flour, salt, baking powder, cinnamon, and nutmeg. In a larger bowl, cream together the butter and honey. Add the buttermilk and eggs, mixing well to blend. Add the dry ingredients along with the blueberries and stir to just moisten. Spoon the batter into the prepared baking pan and bake for 40-45 minutes or until a toothpick inserted into the center comes out clean. Cool on a rack for 10 minutes, then turn out onto a serving plate.

   Make the topping by combining the butter, honey, buttermilk, and cinnamon in a small saucepan. Heat over high to the candy point, a boil that you cannot stir down. Cook for 1 minute, then add the nuts. Cool for a minute or two, then pour over the cake. Cool completely before serving.

The *candy point* is a cooking term that refers to a rapid boil that cannot be stirred down. Sugar or honey is heated with fruit extracts or rinds, or bits of fresh fruit and spices. The mixture is heated to the candy point and cooked for several minutes before being poured over a cake or formed into candy.

Blueberry Muffins

Muffins and a cup of coffee—what a way to begin the day. The fresh blueberries called for in this recipe pop in your mouth with every bite. This simple recipe only requires one bowl, making cleanup a snap.

YIELD: 15 MUFFINS

1 large egg
2 tablespoons canola oil
3/4 cup granulated sugar
1 cup plain nonfat yogurt
2 1/2 cups unbleached flour
1 teaspoon baking powder
1 teaspoon baking soda
1/2 teaspoon salt
1 1/2 cups fresh blueberries

Preheat the oven to 325 degrees F. Whisk the egg and oil together in a large bowl. Add the sugar and stir until smooth. Stir in the yogurt then add the flour, baking powder, baking soda, and salt and stir until just combined. Fold in the blueberries.

Place paper liners into the cups of a muffin tin. Spoon the batter in, filling the cups almost to the top. Bake for 20-25 minutes. Remove from the muffin tin and allow to cool on a rack for about 15 minutes before eating. They will stay fresh for a day or two.

Banana Nut Bread

For a special treat, top a toasted slice with cream cheese, chopped nuts, and a drizzle of honey.

YIELD: 12 SERVINGS

2/3 cup unsalted butter
1/2 cup honey
2 large eggs, beaten
1 1/2 cups mashed ripe banana (about 3 large)
2 3/4 cups whole wheat pastry flour
1 teaspoon baking powder
1 teaspoon baking soda
1/2 teaspoon salt
1/2 cup plain nonfat yogurt
1 cup chopped walnuts

Preheat the oven to 350 degrees F. Butter a large loaf pan and set it aside. In a large bowl, cream together the butter and honey. Stir in the eggs and bananas.

In a separate bowl, sift together the flour, baking powder, baking soda, and salt. Add the dry ingredients alternately with the yogurt to the creamed mixture, blending well after each addition. Stir in the nuts. Spoon the batter into the buttered loaf pan. Bake for 45 to 55 minutes until a toothpick inserted in the center comes out clean. Allow to cool for about 1 hour before removing it from the pan. Cool before slicing.

And the best bread was of my mother's own making— the best in all the land!

—Old Memories by Henry James

Chocolate Cardamom Bundt Cake

Cardamom, a spice frequently used in Indian cooking, adds a unique flavor to this chocolate cake. Serve it with Honey Streaked Latté (page 75), or ice-cold milk. Fresh strawberries or raspberries are a delicious garnish.

YIELD: 16 SERVINGS

2 cups unbleached flour
1/2 cup Dutch process cocoa
2 teaspoons baking soda
1 teaspoon baking powder
1/2 teaspoon ground cardamom
1/4 teaspoon salt
1 1/2 cups granulated sugar
1 cup buttermilk
1/3 cup canola oil
1 cup freshly squeezed orange juice
2 teaspoons orange extract
1 teaspoon powdered sugar

Preheat the oven to 350 degrees F. Lightly oil an 8-cup bundt pan, then dust with about a teaspoon of cocoa powder. Shake out any extra cocoa and set the pan aside.

In a large glass bowl, sift together the flour, cocoa, baking soda, baking powder, cardamom, and salt. Stir in the sugar. Place the buttermilk and oil in a separate glass bowl and stir to combine with a wooden spoon. Stir in the orange juice and orange extract. Make a well in the center of the dry ingredients and add the buttermilk mixture. Beat with a wooden spoon until smooth. Pour the batter into the prepared pan and bake for 50 minutes. Insert a toothpick into the cake. If it comes out clean remove cake from the oven; if batter clings continue to bake for 5 to 10 minutes.

Place the cake on a wire rack to cool in the pan for 20 minutes. Carefully invert the pan onto a cake platter to remove the cake. Place the powdered sugar in a fine mesh wire strainer and dust the cake. Allow to cool completely before serving.

Chocolate not only tastes good, it also provides some important nutrients. Comparatively speaking, a 1.5-ounce chocolate bar supplies more protein, calcium, and riboflavin than snacks like pretzels and potato chips.

Cranberry Scones

Scones come together quickly. Combine the dry ingredients together the night before as an added time saver. Eat the baked scones the same day, or freeze them as described in this chapter. Dried blueberries or currents may be substituted for the cranberries for a delicious variation.

YIELD: 12 SCONES

2 cups unbleached flour
1 tablespoon baking powder
$^1/_4$ teaspoon salt
1 cup buttermilk
2 tablespoons honey, warmed
2 tablespoons Marsala wine
$^1/_3$ cup unsalted butter, melted
$^1/_2$ cup dried cranberries

Preheat the oven to 350 degrees F. Lightly oil a baking sheet and set aside. In a medium bowl, sift together the flour, baking powder, and salt. Set aside.

Place the buttermilk, honey, and Marsala in a large bowl. Whisk together until well blended. Add half of the flour mixture and stir until incorporated. You will have a somewhat lumpy batter at this point. Add the melted butter a little at a time, beating after each addition, creating a smooth batter. Stir in the remaining flour mixture and cranberries until just incorporated. The dough will be stiff and slightly sticky. Turn out onto a floured work surface.

Turn and knead the dough several times, then divide into thirds. Form each third into a uniform thick circle. Cut each circle into quarters and place the resulting wedges on the baking sheet. Bake 20 to 25 minutes until lightly browned.

> Looks can be deceiving—it's
> eating that's believing.
>   —James Thurber

George's Cheese Cake

My friend Dennis Newhall's father, George, is the master cheesecake maker. He has been known to go into the kitchen and whip one up without the least provocation from his wife. This cheese cake is rich and delicious—it may also be topped with your favorite preserves of fruit.

YIELD: 16 SERVINGS

The crust:
1 3/4 cups find graham-cracker crumbs
1/4 cup finely chopped walnuts
1/2 teaspoon ground cinnamon
1/2 cup unsalted butter, melted

The filling:
3 large eggs
16 ounces cream cheese, room temperature
1 cup granulated sugar
1/4 teaspoon salt
2 teaspoons vanilla extract
1/2 teaspoon almond extract
1/2 teaspoon lemon extract
3 cups sour cream

Preheat the oven to 375 degrees F. In a medium bowl, combine the graham cracker crumbs, walnuts, and cinnamon. Drizzle with the melted butter and stir to just moisten. Press

You are as welcome as flowers in May.

–William Shakespeare

the mixture on the bottom and sides of a 9-inch spring-form pan, reserving about $1/3$ cup to sprinkle on the top.

Place the eggs in a large bowl and beat them until light and fluffy. Add the cream cheese, sugar, salt, vanilla, almond, and lemon extracts. Beat with an electric mixer until smooth. Blend in the sour cream, then pour into the prepared crust. Sprinkle with the remaining crumbs. Place in the center of the oven and bake for 35 to 40 minutes, until the filling has set. There should be a slight crack in the surface.

Remove from the oven and place on a rack to cool completely. Cover with foil and refrigerate for 4 to 5 hours. Just before serving, remove the outer ring of the spring-form pan.

Oatmeal and Chocolate Chip Cookies

I love chocolate chip cookies, in all their infinite variations. This recipe incorporates oatmeal, applesauce, and cinnamon—creating a chewy, nutritious treat. Enjoy them with a Sweet Mexican Mocha (page 77) or Chocolate Malted Milk (page 94).

YIELD: 3 DOZEN

¹/₄ cup unsalted butter
1 cup firmly packed light brown sugar
1 large egg, lightly beaten
1 cup unsweetened applesauce
1 teaspoon vanilla extract
2 cups unbleached flour
1 teaspoon baking powder
¹/₂ teaspoon baking soda
¹/₂ teaspoon salt
¹/₂ teaspoon cinnamon
1 cup rolled oats
1 cup semisweet chocolate chips

Preheat the oven to 350 degrees F. Place the butter and sugar in a large bowl and cream together. Add the egg, applesauce, and vanilla and beat well to incorporate. Set aside.

In a separate smaller bowl, mix together the flour, baking powder, baking soda, salt, and cinnamon. Add, a bit at a time, to the butter mixture, beating to combine after each addition. Stir in the oats and chocolate chips. Drop by rounded table-spoons onto a lightly buttered baking sheet. Bake for 12 minutes. Remove from the oven and allow to stand on the sheet for about a minute, then transfer to a rack to cool.

You have to eat oatmeal or you'll dry up. Anybody knows that.

—*Eloise* by Kay Thompson

Espresso Cinnamon Brownies

I love these brownies with an Italian Espresso or, of course, cold milk. Rich vanilla gelato is a indulgent side note.

YIELD: 12 BROWNIES

2 ounces semisweet chocolate
1/2 teaspoon ground cinnamon
1/2 cup unsalted butter, room temperature
2 large eggs, room temperature
3/4 cup granulated sugar
1/2 teaspoon vanilla extract
2/3 cup unbleached flour
1 tablespoon instant espresso powder
1/4 teaspoon baking soda
1/2 cup chopped walnuts

Preheat the oven to 350 degrees F. Lightly butter 10 × 6 × 2-inch oblong glass baking pan. Place the chocolate in a small heavy-bottomed sauce pan and melt over low heat. Add the cinnamon and stir until smooth. Set aside.

Cream together the butter, eggs, and sugar in a medium bowl. Add the vanilla and the melted chocolate and beat well. In a separate bowl, sift together the flour, espresso powder, baking powder, and salt. Add the flour mixture to the creamed mixture and stir until well combined. Stir in the nuts. Pour into the prepared pan and bake 30 to 35 minutes, until a toothpick inserted in the center comes out clean. Cool on a rack, then cut into 2-inch squares.

Tis an ill cook that cannot
lick his own fingers.
—William Shakespeare

Chocolate Walnut Biscotti

Biscotti—the twice-baked Italian cookie—is simply delicious eaten with, and dipped into, coffee. They are also nice for holiday gift giving, especially since you can make them in advance.

YIELD: 3 DOZEN

3 cups unbleached flour
2 teaspoons baking powder
1/8 teaspoon salt
2 large eggs
3/4 cup canola oil
3/4 cup granulated sugar
1 1/2 teaspoons vanilla extract
1 cup chopped walnuts
4 ounces bittersweet chocolate

Preheat the oven to 350 degrees F. In a medium bowl, stir together the flour, baking powder, and salt. Set aside

In a large bowl, combine the eggs, oil, sugar, and vanilla extract. Beat with an electric mixer or wooden spoon until well combined. Add the flour mixture and nuts and stir to combine. Batter will be stiff and slightly sticky.

With floured hands, divide the dough into thirds. Place one third of the dough on a standard ungreased baking sheet

and form into an elongated loaf about 1 inch thick and 3–4 inches wide. It should be of uniform shape and thickness for best results. Flatten the ends of the loaf by pressing in on them with the palm of your hand.

Proceed with the remaining two portions of dough. The loaves should not touch each other, but they can be arranged close together.

Bake for 20–25 minutes. Remove the pan from the oven and let stand 2 to 3 minutes, leaving the oven on. Use a sharp knife to cut the loaves into $1/2$-inch slices. Let stand 5 minutes, then turn the slices down on one cut side. Return to the oven and bake for 5 minutes, remove the pan, and turn the slices over. Bake an additional 5 minutes. Cool the biscotti completely on the pan.

Break the bittersweet chocolate into pieces and place in a medium bowl. Place the bowl in a microwave oven and melt the chocolate on high for about 1 minute. (Each microwave oven is different, so adjust the time accordingly.) The chocolate should be smooth when stirred. Dip one cut side on each slice of biscotti into the chocolate. Place frosted side up on wax paper to dry. Store biscotti in an airtight container for 2 to 3 weeks.

Chocolate Espresso Cake

This is a dense rich, delicious cake. Serve it with vanilla ice cream and freshly brewed coffee.

YIELD: 16 SERVINGS

1 cup granulated sugar
1/2 cup unsalted butter, room temperature
1 teaspoon vanilla
2 large eggs, lightly beaten
1 1/2 cups unbleached flour
2 tablespoons espresso powder
2 teaspoons baking powder
3/4 teaspoon salt
2/3 cup lowfat milk
1/3 cup Dutch process cocoa

Preheat the oven to 350 degrees F. Lightly oil an 8-cup bundt pan or an 8 × 8 × 2 square pan and set it aside. Cream together the sugar and butter. Add the vanilla and eggs and beat until light and fluffy.

In a separate bowl, sift together the flour, espresso powder, baking powder, and salt. Add this to the creamed mixture alternately with the milk, beating after each addition. Spoon half of the batter into the bundt pan. Add the cocoa to the remaining batter and stir to incorporate. The resulting batter will be very thick. Spoon this evenly into the bundt pan. Insert a knife vertically into the batter and stir slightly to produce a swirl pattern.

Bake for 35 minutes, or until a toothpick inserted into the center comes out clean. Cool for 5 minutes, then turn out of the pan onto a serving plate. Dust with powdered sugar, if desired. Cool completely before slicing.

In 1492, upon his return voyage from America, Columbus presented the Court of King Ferdinand with a treasure trove of many strange and wondrous things. A few dark brown cocoa beans were among his booty, but they seemed quite unpromising. It was not until 1528, when Cortez returned to Spain, that the potential of cocoa became recognized.

Index

These are not exact equivalents: they have been slightly rounded to make measuring easier.

LIQUID MEASUREMENTS

American	Imperial	Metric	Australian
2 tablespoons (1 oz.)	1 fl. oz.	30 ml	1 tablespoon
1/4 cup (2 oz.)	2 fl. oz.	60 ml	2 tablespoons
1/3 cup (3 oz.)	3 fl. oz.	80 ml	1/4 cup
1/2 cup (4 oz.)	4 fl. oz.	125 ml	1/3 cup
2/3 cup (5 oz.)	5 fl. oz.	165 ml	1/2 cup
3/4 cup (6 oz.)	6 fl. oz.	185 ml	2/3 cup
1 cup (8 oz.)	8 fl. oz.	250 ml	3/4 cup

SPOON MEASUREMENTS

American	Metric
1/4 teaspoon	1 ml
1/2 teaspoon	2 ml
1 teaspoon	5 ml
1 tablespoon	15 ml

WEIGHTS

US/UK	Metric
1 oz.	30 grams (g)
2 oz.	60 g
4 oz. (1/4 lb)	125 g
5 oz. (1/3 lb)	155 g
6 oz.	185 g
7 oz.	220 g
8 oz. (1/2 lb)	250 g
10 oz.	315 g
12 oz. (3/4 lb)	375 g
14 oz.	440 g
16 oz. (1 lb)	500 g
2 lbs	1 kg

OVEN TEMPERATURES

Farenheit	Centigrade	Gas
250	120	1/2
300	150	2
325	160	3
350	180	4
375	190	5
400	200	6
450	230	8